BITS, BYTES,
AND BIG BROTHER

Recent Titles in the
Praeger Series in Political Communication
Robert E. Denton, Jr., *General Editor*

Studies in Media and the Persian Gulf War
Edited by Robert E. Denton, Jr.

The Modern Presidency and Crisis Rhetoric
Edited by Amos Kiewe

Governmental Commission Communication
Edited by Christine M. Miller and Bruce C. McKinney

The Presidential Campaign Film: A Critical History
Joanne Morreale

High-Tech Campaigns: Computer Technology in Political Communication
Gary W. Selnow

Rhetorical Studies of National Political Debates: 1960–1992
Edited by Robert V. Friedenberg

Campaigns and Conscience: The Ethics of Political Journalism
Philip Seib

The White House Speaks: Presidential Leadership as Persuasion
Craig Allen Smith and Kathy B. Smith

Public Diplomacy and International Politics: The Symbolic Constructs of
Summits and International Radio News
Robert S. Fortner

The 1992 Presidential Campaign: A Communication Perspective
Edited by Robert E. Denton, Jr.

The 1992 Presidential Debates in Focus
Edited by Diana B. Carlin and Mitchell S. McKinney

Public Relations Inquiry as Rhetorical Criticism: Case Studies of Corporate
Discourse and Social Influence
Edited by William N. Elwood

BITS, BYTES, AND BIG BROTHER

Federal Information Control
in the Technological Age

SHANNON E. MARTIN

Praeger Series in Political Communication

Westport, Connecticut
London

Library of Congress Cataloging-in-Publication Data

Martin, Shannon E.
    Bits, bytes, and big brother : federal information control in the
technological age / Shannon E. Martin.
        p.   cm.—(Praeger series in political communication, ISSN 1062–5623)
    Includes bibliographical references and index.
    ISBN 0–275–94900–1 (alk. paper)
    1. Telematics—Law and legislation—United States. 2. Computers—
Law and legislation—United States. 3. Information technology—
Government policy—United States. I. Title. II. Series.
    KF2765.M37   1995
    343.7309′99—dc20
    [347.303999]   94–32929

British Library Cataloguing in Publication Data is available.

Library of Congress Catalog Card Number: 94–32929
ISBN: 0–275–94900–1
ISSN: 1062–5623

First published in 1995

Praeger Publishers, 88 Post Road West, Westport, CT 06881
An imprint of Greenwood Publishing Group, Inc.

Printed in the United States of America

The paper used in this book complies with the
Permanent Paper Standard issued by the National
Information Standards Organization (Z39.48–1984).

10 9 8 7 6 5 4 3 2

Contents

Series Foreword *by Robert E. Denton, Jr.*   vii

Preface   xi

Introduction
Preliminary Considerations of Information Access
and Control   1

Chapter 1
Brief History of Affirmative Federal Public Access Law   7

Chapter 2
Definitions of 'Information'   19

Chapter 3
The Foreign Agents Registration Act   35

Chapter 4
The Computer Security Act of 1987   55

Chapter 5
The Pentagon Rules on Media Access   71

Chapter 6
Principles of Ethical Reasoning   85

Chapter 7
  Ethical Principles in Federal Information Control   99

Chapter 8
  Federal Information Control in a Technological Age   111

Appendix A
  The Foreign Agents Registration and Propaganda Act   117

Appendix B
  The Computer Security Act of 1987   137

Appendix C
  Media Pools in the Persian Gulf 1991   147

Selected Bibliography   155

Index   163

Series Foreword

Those of us from the discipline of communication studies have long believed that communication is prior to all other fields of inquiry. In several other forums I have argued that the essence of politics is "talk" or human interaction.[1] Such interaction may be formal or informal, verbal or nonverbal, public or private but it is always persuasive, forcing us consciously or subconsciously to interpret, to evaluate, and to act. Communication is the vehicle for human action.

From this perspective, it is not surprising that Aristotle recognized the natural kinship of politics and communication in his writings *Politics* and *Rhetoric*. In the former, he establishes that humans are "political beings [who] alone of the animals [are] furnished with the faculty of language."[2] And in the latter, he begins his systematic analysis of discourse by proclaiming that "rhetorical study, in its strict sense, is concerned with the modes of persuasion."[3] Thus, it was recognized over 2,300 years ago that politics and communication go hand in hand because they are essential parts of human nature.

Back in 1981, Dan Nimmo and Keith Sanders proclaimed that political communication was an emerging field.[4] Although its origin, as noted, dates back centuries, a "self-consciously cross-disciplinary" focus began in the late 1950s. Thousands of books and articles later, colleges and universities offer a variety of graduate and undergraduate coursework in such diverse departments as communication, mass communication, journalism, political science and sociology.[5] In Nimmo and Sanders' early assessment, the "key areas of inquiry" included rhetorical analysis, propaganda analysis, attitude change studies, voting studies, government and the news media, functional and systems analyses, technological changes, media technologies, campaign techniques, and research techniques.[6] In a survey of the state of the field in 1983, the same authors and Lynda Kaid found additional, more specific areas of concerns such as the presidency, political polls, public opinion, debates, and advertising to name a few.[7] Since the first study, they also noted a shift away from the rather strict behavioral approach.

A decade later, Dan Nimmo and David Swanson argued that "political communication has developed some identity as a more or less distinct domain of scholarly work."[8] The scope and concerns of the area have further expanded to include critical theories and cultural studies. While there is no precise definition, method, or disciplinary home of the area of inquiry, its primary domain is the role, processes, and effects of communication within the context of politics broadly defined.

In 1985, the editors of *Political Communication Yearbook: 1984* noted that "more things are happening in the study, teaching, and practice of political communication than can be captured within the space limitations of the relatively few publications available."[9] In addition, they argued that the backgrounds of "those involved in the field [are] so varied and pluralist in outlook and approach, . . . it [is] a mistake to adhere slavishly to any set format in shaping the content."[10] And more recently, Nimmo and Swanson called for "ways of overcoming the unhappy consequences of fragmentation within a framework that respects, encourages, and benefits from diverse scholarly commitments, agendas, and approaches."[11]

In agreement with these assessments of the area and with gentle encouragement, Praeger established in 1988 the Praeger Series in Political Communication. The series is open to all qualitative and quantitative methodologies as well as contemporary and historical studies. The key to characterizing the studies in the series is the focus on communication variables or activities within a political context or dimension. As of this writing, nearly forty volumes have been published and there are numerous impressive works forthcoming. Scholars from the disciplines of communication, history, journalism, political science, and sociology have participated in the series.

I am, without shame or modesty, a fan of the series. The joy of serving as its editor is in participating in the dialogue of the field of political communication and in reading the contributors' works. I invite you to join me.

Robert E. Denton, Jr.

NOTES

1. See Robert E. Denton, Jr., *The Symbolic Dimensions of the American Presidency* (Prospect Heights, Ill.: Waveland Press, 1982); Robert E. Denton, Jr., and Gary Woodward, *Political Communication in America* (N.Y.: Praeger, 1985; 2nd ed., 1990); Robert E. Denton, Jr., and Dan Hahn, *Presidential Communication* (New York: Praeger, 1986); and Robert E. Denton, Jr., *The Primetime Presidency of Ronald Reagan* (New York: Praeger, 1988).

2. Aristotle, *The Politics of Aristotle*, trans. Ernest Barker (New York: Oxford University Press, 1970), p. 5.

3. Aristotle, *Rhetoric*, trans. Rhys Roberts (New York: The Modern Library, 1954), p. 22.

4. Dan Nimmo and Keith Sanders, "Introduction: The Emergence of Political Communication as a Field," in *Handbook of Political Communication*, ed. Dan Nimmo and Keith Sanders (Beverly Hills, Calif.: Sage, 1981), pp. 11-36.

5. Ibid., p. 15.

6. Ibid., pp. 17-27.

7. Keith Sanders, Lynda Kaid, and Dan Nimmo, eds., *Political Communication Yearbook: 1984* (Carbondale: Southern Illinois University, 1985), pp. 283-308.

8. Dan Nimmo and David Swanson, "The Field of Political Communication: Beyond the Voter Persuasion Paradigm," in *New Directions in Political Communication*, ed. David Swanson and Dan Nimmo (Beverly Hills, Calif.: Sage, 1990), p. 8.

9. Sanders, Kaid, and Nimmo, *Political Communication Yearbook: 1984*, p. xiv.

10. Ibid.

11. Nimmo and Swanson, "The Field of Political Communication," p. 11.

Preface

The most fundamental rules among social beings are the moral principles on which each society frames its laws. Those moral principles are often left unarticulated, but they may be inferred through the kinds of laws a government imposes on its citizens during the life of the social order. The moral principles on which the governmental frame was built are somewhat obscure, though the United States is fortunate to have a cache of founding documents produced over a relatively short period of time and by intellectuals who were well-acquainted contemporaries.

Through the first century of the country's life the national spirit of the United States carried the social order while refinements were made. During the nation's second century, the moral underpinnings seemed at times obscured or confused by an expanding array of newly developing moral models. Deontological and teleological models mingled and tugged at the evolving social order where once there were primarily deontological morals only. These moral developments seemed to create a need for new laws. But the moral underpinnings seemed now less coherently shared among the electorate.

As the country moves into its third century, there is a need to look again at the evolution of the moral models on which the nation wants to build a modern frame for laws governing that key element necessary for a working democracy—information. The U.S. government is reported to be the largest producer and distributor of information in the world. Control of all that data is a monumental task for government administration. As well, understanding and developing the kinds of controls necessary and desirable for all that valuable information have been constant concerns of many who interact with and within the government.

The subject of this book is a review of three specific federal information control actions in light of the moral principles evident in the Declaration of Independence and the Constitution. The work here is intended to aid a national dialogue about how the electorate wants the government to work in their information interests. More generally, the work here compares the 18th century founding framers' First Amendment principles, that protected the nation's early information avenues, to the three 20th century information control examples, where the modern framers are reshaping and redefining information byways as the nation enters the 21st century.

Special thanks must go to Edwin A. Martin for constant and consistent help throughout the project, from development of the ideas all the way through completion of this work. He gave unfailing attention as well as technical support when asked, at any hour of the day or night. Thanks, too, go to Donald L. Shaw, Stephanie Haas, Ed Holley and Phil Meyer at the University of North Carolina-Chapel Hill and Andrews Reath at North Carolina State who encouraged the author's developing scholarship, and Margaret Blanchard, also at UNC-Chapel Hill, who encouraged the author's enthusiasm for and pursuit of research. Duane Stoltzfus, at Rutgers University, deserves thanks, for taking on the task of checking the author's research citations in this work, and to Richard Hixson, also at Rutgers, for listening to developments and suggesting refinements in the work. Thanks, also, go to David Auerbach, Mary Rossi and Ann Rives for their assistance in the book's production.

BITS, BYTES,
AND BIG BROTHER

Introduction: Preliminary Considerations of Information Access and Control

One premise of the form of government adopted by the United States is that information about government must flow freely, or at least be easily accessible, to citizens in order for the electorate to make well-informed decisions. There is, however, a long-observed tension in the United States between the citizen's need to be informed about government's activities and the government's desire to keep secret that information it has collected for effective governing.[1] That tension is often increased when, for example, citizens seek access to government-held information during periods of heightened distress such as war with foreign governments, domestic unrest, or severe economic hardship.[2] Government's felt need for secrecy often increases during such crises, even though—it has been suggested by some scholars—it is at these very times that citizens most need to be well informed about government-held information.[3]

During the 1980s, when the U.S. government was not engaged in a declared war with a strong foreign government, threatened by domestic social unrest or facing a national economic depression, the executive branch of the federal government chose to initiate subtle, substantial roadblocks to avenues of access for those seeking government-held information. These efforts included a renewed use of the Foreign Agents Registration and Propaganda Act[4] that was reviewed by Congress for possible amendment several times during the past decade, the successful passage of the Computer Security Act of 1987[5] and the strict enforcement of media pools during the 1991 Persian Gulf military strike.[6] All three of these government actions in essence controlled and often slowed or significantly interrupted the flow of information, to which some citizens thought they had a right of access.

ACCESS AND CONTROL

In the 20th century, the U.S. Congress has explicitly acted twice in strong support of the premise that free-flowing information from government to citizens is a necessary condition of self-governance in this country. These statutes include the Freedom of Information Act[7] and the Depository Library Program.[8] Supporters of the Freedom of Information Act and the Depository Library Program often cited the 'right' of public access to government information.[9] And the United States Constitution's First Amendment principles are often coupled with this 'right' of public access.[10] But the coupling of these rights is not to be found in the language of the First Amendment, which represents only what Congress shall not do, rather than what citizens have a right to do. As is more fully discussed in the chapter on public access law, many legislators assumed that citizens should have access to government-held information, and so provided documents as a matter of routine.

When legislators have thought that citizens' rights were being eroded, they have occasionally looked to positivist remedies—that is, constructing law in support of the supposed rights. The Freedom of Information Act and the Depository Library Program might be thought of in this way. The success of these remedies, however, has been less than overwhelming. And it could be that a different view of constructing remedies should be sought.

It is at this point that the similarities between talk about First Amendment rights, and rights of public access to government-held information meet. Just as the First Amendment's negativist language may be reconstructed to support rights of free expression,[11] perhaps negativist language about government information control may serve as a construction to support rights of public access to government-held information.[12]

THREE RECENT GOVERNMENT ACTIONS

The three government actions reviewed in this book are the Foreign Agents Registration Act (FARA), the Computer Security Act

(CSA) and the Pentagon Rules for Media Access to the Persian Gulf War (Pentagon Media Rules). Two of these are statutory laws (FARA and CSA), meaning that they are laws passed by Congress. The Pentagon Rules on Media Access to the Persian Gulf War are administrative law, meaning that Congress has delegated this area of law-making, either explicitly or traditionally, to the executive branch of the U.S. government. In this case, media management that involves the military is usually handled by the executive branch, and Congress chose not to alter that pattern in 1991 while George Bush was President and Commander in Chief.

All three of these government actions affect information flow, but none defines 'information.' All three were instigated by the executive branch, subsequently assisted by Congress, and have been the subject of congressional review within the past ten years. The Foreign Agents Registration Act and the Computer Security Act were enacted by Congress after executive branch instigation and initial bill origination. The Pentagon Media Rules were administrative law that was relinquished by Congress to the executive branch, and not actively contradicted or superseded by Congress.

INFORMATION FLOW

The Foreign Agents Registration Act was initially enacted to monitor information brought into the United States by foreigners and made available to United States citizens. The Computer Security Act was enacted to protect information that moves within the U.S. computer data base systems and into the information stream available to U.S. citizens. And the media pools initiated through the Persian Gulf War administrative rule were intended to control information that might be gathered by U.S. citizens about U.S. involvement in an offshore conflict.

These three examples, then, describe a variety of information flow models:

1. information, moved or carried by outsiders (non-U.S. citizens), coming into the United States (FARA);

2. information, moved by insiders (U.S. citizens within the United States), remaining within the United States (CSA);

3. information by insiders (U.S. citizens who are outside the United States), coming into the United States (Pentagon Media Rules).

A thorough review of the congressional and executive branch documents relevant to FARA, CSA and the Pentagon Media Rules is necessary in order to understand on what grounds Congress and the executive branch sought to control the information flow in these separate arenas. During the review of documents, some central issues will recur as well. These concerns include the following:

1. A consistent understanding and use of the term 'information' by those interested in controlling it;

2. A consistent support of free-flowing information;

3. A consistent philosophical underpinning for exceptions to the premise that free-flowing information is a necessary condition for successful self-governance in the United States.

If the review of these particular laws—FARA, CSA and the Pentagon Media Rules—suggests there is confusion about the concept of information, it would be useful to sort through the variety of understandings found in the government documents, and organize them into some set of categories so that the specific problems created by laws affecting information flow can be usefully addressed. If there is confusion about the concept of information among those writing and administering statute and administrative law that controls information flow, then the traditional principle of supporting information flow will probably be undermined by the law's language, and ultimately perhaps, by the administration of the law.

The renewed interest in the Foreign Agents Registration Act, the passage of the Computer Security Act and the congressional support of the Pentagon Rules on Media Access to the Persian Gulf War provide a variety of venues for researching government understandings of information, flow and control,[13] as well as the reasons government may provide for inhibiting U.S. citizens' access to government-held information. These particular examples are significant, too, because they may suggest a shift in controlling the flow of information—from the legislature to the executive branch—at a time that no real national emergency existed which might naturally prompt such a shift, the kind of shift often observed during periods of war and national distress.[14]

The specific points first to be made, then, must be

1. the evidence that a belief in the traditional premise of information flow does exist;

2. the existence of statutes exemplifying such a premise;

3. and the kinds of definitions of 'information' and 'control' necessary for an examination of government action specifically affecting information flow.

If, then, it becomes clear in the course of this examination that there is a move by the government away from the traditional reasons for and principles underpinning free-flowing information from government to citizens, then citizens can begin consciously to construct, or reconstruct, those principles that inform the government now mapping the information superhighways.

Finally, then, it is important to construct a set of principles on which government frames these information controls and which the electorate might deem appropriate. The development of a principled frame for information control is the concluding phase of this book. It is intended to provide suggestions and act as an initiation point for serious work that is urgently necessary if the nation hopes to move successfully into the 21st century.

NOTES

1. See Vincent Blasi, "The Checking Value in First Amendment Theory," *American Bar Foundation Research Journal* 1977:523; Frederick Schauer, *Free Speech: A Philosophical Enquiry* (N.Y.: Cambridge University Press, 1982) and Zechariah Chafee, Jr., *Free Speech in the United States* (N.Y.: Atheneum, 1969) (1941).

2. See Margaret Blanchard, *Revolutionary Sparks: Freedom of Expression in Modern America* (N.Y.: Oxford University Press, 1992).

3. For example, see statements by Frederick Schauer and Jeanne Woods, *Foreign Communication Free Trade Act of 1989: Hearings Before the Subcomm. on Courts, Intellectual Property and the Administration of Justice, H.R. Comm. on the Judiciary*, 101st Cong., 2d Sess. (March 29, 1990).

4. 22 U.S.C. 611 (1992).

5. Pub.L.No. 100-235, 101 Stat.1724.

6. See Ron Wildermuth, memo dated August 1990, "Annex Foxtrot." Wildermuth was General H. Norman Schwarzkopf's chief public relations representative at U.S. Central Command in Tampa, Florida, reported in *Pentagon Rules on Media Access to the Persian Gulf War*, Hearing before the Committee on Governmental Affairs, Senate Hearing 102-178, February 20, 1991, p. 279.

7. *Freedom of Information Act*, 5 U.S.C. 552 (1992).

8. *Depository Library Act of 1962*, Pub.L.No.87-579, 76 Stat. 352 (1962).

9. See, for instance, "Principles of Public Information: A Major Federal Policy Document from the National Commission On Libraries and Information

Science (NCLIS)," *Information Hotline*, 22:5 (October 1990); "Government Documents Roundtable (GODORT) Principles on Government Information," *Documents to the People* 19:12 (March 1991); Fred H. Cate, D. Annette Fields and James K. McBain, "The Right to Privacy and the Public's Right to Know: The 'Central Purpose' of the Freedom of Information Act," *Administrative Law Review* 46:41 (Winter 1994).

10. See, for instance, Ulkrika Ekman Ault, "The FBI's Library Awareness Program: Is Big Brother Reading Over Your Shoulder?" *New York University Law Review* 65:1532 (December 1990).

11. Ruth Walden, "A Government Action Approach to First Amendment Analysis," *Journalism Quarterly* 69(1):65 (Spring 1992).

12. Information access, control and censorship should not be thought of as interchangeable terms in this book. Here information access will mean the opportunity, or lack there of, to acquire information, whereas censorship will mean impairing distribution of information already acquired. Censorship and information control can, of course, bring about the same result so that censorship could be thought of as a form of information control. However, attention in this book will be specifically about those activities that actually bar access to information—those that deny initial opportunities to achieve, grasp or aquire information.

13. Information control here refers to monitoring and manipulating information flow, and not just to keeping secrets.

14. See Christopher Dunn, "Judging Secrets," *Villanova Law Review* 31:471 (1986), for a similar suggestion of judicial/executive branch balance.

Chapter 1

Brief History of Affirmative Federal Public Access Law

Among the premises of the organization of U.S. government are two that directly affect distribution of information about government. They are (1) that the government serves the citizens, and (2) that a well-informed constituency is a prerequisite for giving direction to those government members who act on behalf of the citizens,[1] for holding government accountable,[2] and for checking government corruption.[3] It is therefore of particular importance that the government's constituency be informed about government actions and activities. As 18th century philosopher Adam Smith had suggested, the "ideal observer" of government was one who was "fully informed, free, . . .willing to universalize, . . . considering the good of everyone alike."[4]

There is a history of some restrictions being applied to the time, place and manner of exchanges in the free marketplace of ideas, but the intent of these is not to close off the exchange of information but to guard against disorder.[5] Since the U.S. Constitution was ratified two hundred years ago, the federal legislature has acted in two arenas to explicitly ensure that citizens are provided published[6] information about government operations. Those two arenas have resulted in the Depository Library Program,[7] and the Freedom of Information Act[8] and related subsequent Sunshine Laws.[9]

The intentions of Congress were clear and unified in these legislative actions. A review of the congressional hearings and the specific language of the laws describing the Depository Library Program (DLP) and the Freedom of Information Act (FOIA) points clearly to a history of legislators plainly declaring every citizen's right of access to material generated either by the government or for the government.

DEPOSITORY LIBRARY PROGRAM

During the early sessions of the Continental Congress a resolution was passed that directed the publishing and distribution of copies of the new laws as well as the Congress' *Journals*,[10] which detailed the results of the legislature's deliberations. Distribution was primarily to the states' legislative and executive branch offices and to the delegates, who then distributed the laws to other appropriate locations within their districts. In addition, the Continental Congress specifically noted in 1784 that complete copies of congressional material should be provided to the Library Company of Philadelphia.[11] Congress regularly directed that material generated during sessions or provided to it for review also be printed and distributed for public consumption.[12]

Publication and distribution of legislative material continued without interruption, though some bumps and hurdles frustrated the effort. For instance, printing costs increased because the number of copies needed increased as the population grew.[13] Distribution costs, too, increased as the population of the country spread westward. Noted in the legislature's records was the observation that "in a country so extensive as America, and where the people are so widely scattered, it was a work of immense difficulty to have a regular and accurate account of the measures of Government communicated through every part of the Union."[14] These problems were soon joined by the in-house difficulty of specifying which documents were "government publications."[15] The presumption, however, among congressional delegates was that public access to government material was in part a responsibility of the government. The cost and difficulty of preparation, publication and distribution were the burden of government bodies, not of the citizens desiring to be informed.

The 19th century patchwork of resolutions and paperwork that provided for public access to government-held information does not suggest that the cost of production and provision be passed on directly to recipients of the information. But Congress was becoming more and more burdened with the necessity of a resolution specifying who received the contract, how many copies, at what cost, and to whom the copies would go. In addition, it was not always clear exactly when there was a need for the printing of documents. So in 1895 Congress decided instead to provide continually for publication of government documents through The Printing Act.[16] The act provided for a single government publishing office and an all-encompassing directive on the distribution of congressional publications to designated offices and public facilities; among these facilities were depository libraries.[17]

Revisions of the law[18] now referred to as the Depository Library Act (DLA) during the 1960s included modifications in definitions, but there were no substantial changes in the intent of the original legislation.[19] Provisions of Title 44 of the *United States Code*, Chapter 19, designate the establishment and operation of depository libraries under the direction of the Superintendent of Documents. Documents shall include the following: journals of the Senate and House of Representatives; all publications, not confidential in character, printed upon the requisition of a congressional committee; Senate and House public bills and resolutions; and reports on private bills, concurrent or simple resolutions.[20]

The DLA is founded on three principles: (1) with certain specified exceptions, all government publications shall be made available to depository libraries; (2) depository libraries shall be located in each state and congressional district in order to make government publications widely available; and (3) these government publications shall be available for the free use of the general public.[21] While as many as three depository libraries may be located in any congressional district, "where it [the library] can best serve the public need,"[22] the cost of each facility and service of the collection must be borne by the library itself, either through local government funding or under private auspices. There were, in the early 1990s, about 1,400 designated depository libraries.

The intention of the law is to provide free and convenient access to government information through a program of libraries established throughout the United States. While the bulk of the material for publication emanates specifically from Congress, information about other branches of government provided to Congress in the form of reports and hearings material is part of that cache.

FREEDOM OF INFORMATION ACT

The history of the Freedom of Information Act (FOIA) occurs in a much shorter period than the Depository Library Program but is also well documented. The FOIA was born during the mid-1950s when U.S. Congressman John Moss, Jr. (Democrat-California) headed a sub-committee investigating charges that government agencies were with-holding information about their activities that was, among other things, necessary for members of Congress to perform their duties.[23] Moss became increasingly frustrated and angry with the executive branch's uncooperativeness about public access to government business during the decade of his investigations. At his urging, in 1966 the legis-lature enacted the FOIA,[24] which applies only to federal government agencies and not to state or local bodies.

While the legislation does not include a statement of purpose, the Senate report accompanying the bill declared that the FOIA is to "establish a general philosophy of full agency disclosure."[25] Passage of the FOIA established a statutory right of access to government information "to ensure an informed citizenry, vital to the functioning of a democratic society, needed to check against corruption and to hold the governors accountable to the governed."[26]

The FOIA was an active assertion by Congress of the federal government's responsibility to provide information to interested citizens. While the original legislation provided for some areas of government operations that might require temporary secrecy—such as national security and law enforcement interests—the bill presumed that it was the federal government's burden to prepare and provide information about agencies' business sought by citizens.[27]

The FOIA contains nine exemptions to a statutory right of access. These exemptions, briefly, include material designated by the executive branch as restricted for national security reasons, certain law enforce-ment agency records, personnel records or medical records that contain confidential information, certain banking records, trade secrets records, internal agency memoranda, geological or geophysical data on oil and gas wells, and any material explicitly exempted by an act of Congress. But apart from these exceptions, all federal government records are assumed to be public information, available upon request.

During the three decades since the FOIA's enactment hundreds of suits have been filed against agencies for non-compliance. Interpreta-tion by the courts of the legislation has provided much legal detail, but has also pointed out the wide array of questions that still surround assertions of a citizen's right to know specific facts about that govern-ment which the citizen supports. The Supreme Court has suggested a "citizen's right to know"[28] in principle but has never explicitly recognized a broad-based constitutional right to know.[29] Congress' statutory declaration of a "right to know" exemplified by the FOIA is, however, recognized by the courts and tested in the balancing of statutory law, rather than on purely constitutional grounds.[30]

In summary, then, Congress has acted at least twice on behalf of citizens explicitly to provide published information about the government for the governed. The first of these actions was the DLA covering congressional materials. The second action was the FOIA covering all governmental agencies, including some agencies in the executive branch. But both statutory regulations are founded on substantially the same principle—that an informed citizenry is paramount to a well-functioning representative democracy.

INHIBITORS

Roadblocks to public access of information about government exist, however, in numbers great enough to have sparked a renewed debate about the underlying principles as well as the specific instances. In the mid-1980s the American Library Association convened the Commission on Freedom and Equality of Access to Information chaired by Dan M. Lacy.[31] The commission members included not only academic and practicing librarians but also publishers, lawyers and industry specialists.[32] Their charge was to define the issues that modern technology thrust upon the information industry, and to provide specific policy suggestions for the government.[33] They noted that there had been increased pressure for curtailment or withdrawal of federal support of information access programs and institutions, and that there had also been substantial federal efforts to limit and control information flow from the government.[34]

In response, the commission recommended that the Freedom of Information Act be preserved and strengthened, not diminished. More specifically, the commission recommended that greater openness in government would be promoted by limiting security classification exemptions to significant areas of national security and by curtailing all abuses of security classification. The commission concluded, "The recent set of strictures against the flow of government information limits the ability of citizens to make informed judgments about public policy. What is needed is a consistent public policy to maximize the availability of information from the government to its citizens."[35]

Members of Congress also called for renewed support for the principles supporting the citizen's right to know. The *Congressional Record* of March 4, 1988, contains a tribute to James Madison on the anniversary of his birth. The day was proclaimed Freedom of Information Day, and the attending statement by Sen. Paul Simon was titled "The Right to Know: Preserving Self-Government and Public Accountability." Similarly, Rep. Lee Hamilton called for a serious review of the information classification system and its uses in a 1989 statement he made, titled "Government Secrecy" and reported in the *Record* on February 9, 1989.

But by the early 1990s, the DLA was subject to an executive branch administrative directive[36] requiring a cost-benefit analysis of information supplied to patrons, and stressing a shift in reliance to private sector suppliers of such information. The directive also suggested that cost recovery for the information services be through user fees. The FOIA was also subject to a broader executive branch interpretation of national security restrictions[37] and the court has been narrowing its interpretation of the statutory parameters.[38]

Additional problems for the DLA also arose with the government's increased use of computer-generated and computer-stored information. Many depository libraries found it difficult to purchase and maintain the level and quality of hardware and software required for access to the government's computer-held data. There were also increasing problems for DLA users and the FOIA requesters concerning how to translate the computer-held material once it was received by the non-expert citizen.

The FOIA requesters experienced increased delays from agencies, and charges for the hours agency employees spent retrieving and copying the materials. All of these problems distill to basic concerns over additional cost and difficulty of access for citizens who try to retrieve public information—information they have, in a sense, already paid for initially through taxes, and to which they are entitled by congressional mandate.

Again, the original legislative assumption of the DLP and the FOIA was that government is responsible for providing information to citizens about its business. The federal government is reported to be the single largest consumer and distributor of information in the world.[39] Decisions made in government agencies about the kind of information, and the manner in which the information will be stored greatly affect future access for both DPL users and FOIA requests. In a

1989 article, the depository librarians decried their problems as the "exponential increase in the amount of depository material and the variety of formats [supplied by the government] added to the limited resources of regional depositories, staff, space, funding, online searching, travel telecommunication and equipment."[40] Clearly the concern here is with both form and content, the compilation of which creates a nightmare of inaccessibility for the librarian and public information seeker.

Congress, in an effort to minimize the burden of federal paperwork on citizens and "minimize the cost to the federal government of collecting, maintaining, using, and disseminating information,"[41] passed the Paperwork Reduction Act.[42] Under the auspices of this legislation, the Office of Management initiated Circular A-130, previously noted, suggesting that government agencies, including depository libraries, consider cost management alternatives to currently maintained records and materials. To achieve cost savings for the printing and distributing of information to library users, A-130 suggests that DLP librarians shift, whenever possible, citizens' requests to private-sector suppliers of government information.

Similarly, the FOIA officers have been directed by the executive branch to supply minimum information[43] and courts are supporting those directives.[44] Since the FOIA officer is an employee of the federal agency receiving a FOIA request, the employee's greatest allegiance might rest with the agency. This kind of situation, then, is an additional concern for the FOIA requester whose only contact with an agency is not through a friendly or sympathetic agent. In both the DLP and the FOIA users' experience, however, the net result is the same—frustration. The user is faced with a roadblock in the form of either a dearth of data or vacuum of inaccessible information; the source of this roadblock is a subtle government initiative that clearly is unconcerned about any obligation or responsibility to provide for an informed citizenry.

Apart from sheer quantity, or lack, of information provided by the government is the problem of the information's form. Computerization in government records increased from about 3,000 computers at the time of the FOIA passage, to about 48,000 mainframe computers in 1990.[45] Similarly, use of smaller microcomputers more than doubled during a scant two year period to more than a million units by 1989.[46] And, in fact, when the National Institute of Standards and Technology tried to survey all of the computers in use by the federal government for any level of restricted information work, they were unable to reach a conclusive figure.[47]

As noted earlier, the range of computer hardware and software in use has created access problems for DLP librarians. FOIA requesters experience similar frustration. A 1989 article chronicles the kinds of roadblocks the FOIA requester experiences in the labyrinth of unfamiliar software.[48] The FOIA requester repeatedly finds that a computer system may become a "black hole for information that would otherwise be accessible under the FOIA."[49]

This computerization problem ultimately revolves around the issue of just how much right the DLP user or a FOIA requester has to computerized information. The DLP user clearly has the right to use whatever material is supplied to the depository library, but the FOIA requester still faces the difficulty of convincing a sometimes less-than-sympathetic FOIA officer that computer-held information is not off-limits.[50] Similarly, there is still some question whether the DLA encompasses electronic information at all.[51]

Finally, charges for services to users of both the FOIA and the DLA have been suggested as a deterrent to casual use. In fact, the FOIA requester already pays for search time and copies at a rate set by the agency.[52] Exceptions are made, but granted grudgingly.[53] In contrast, the possibility of charging users has been hotly debated among depository librarians.[54] Ultimately the depository librarian membership of the American Library Association recommended against user charges,[55] but the Office of Government Printing may have the last word.[56]

NOTES

1. See Leonard W. Levy, *Essays on the Making of the Constitution* (New York: Oxford University Press, 1987); Sarah Jordan Miller, *The Depository Library System: A History* (Columbia University dissertation, 1980); *A Directory of U.S. Government Depository Libraries* (S. Prt. 100-127, 100th Congress, 2d sess., October 1988).

2. Zechariah Chafee, Jr., *Free Speech in the United States* (N.Y.: Atheneum, 1969).

3. Vincent Blasi, "The Checking Value in First Amendment Theory," *American Bar Foundation Research Journal* 1977: 523.

4. Quoted by Alan Gewirth, *Reason and Morality* (Chicago: University of Chicago Press, 1978) p. 20.

5. *Grayned v. City of Rockford*, 408 U.S. 104 (1972) provides some insight

on time, place and manner regulation.

6. Burt A. Braverman and Frances J. Chetwynd, *Information Law: Freedom of Information, Privacy, Open Meetings, Other Access Laws* (N.Y.: Practising Law Institute, 1985) p.75ff 2 §3.1-3.8.

7. 44 U.S.C. §19 (1991).

8. 5 U.S.C. §552 (1991).

9. 5 U.S.C. §552b (1991).

10. *Journals*, ed. in the Library of Congress, (September 26, 1776) 5: 829; (June 2, 1777) 8: 412.

11. Miller, *The Depository Library System: A History*, 36.

12. Miller, 29.

13. Miller, 46.

14. *Annals* 4, 3d Cong., 2d sess., 951 (December 1, 1794).

15. Miller, *The Depository Library System: A History*, 50.

16. 28 Stat. 601 (1895).

17. 28 Stat. 624 (1895).

18. *Depository Library Act of 1962*, Pub.L. No.87-579, 76 Stat. 352 (1962).

19. Codified in *Title 44*.

20. 44 U.S.C. §1903.

21. *A Directory of U.S. Government Depository Libraries*, S.Prt. 100-127, 100th Cong. 2d sess. (1988).

22. 44 U.S.C. §1909.

23. *Availability of the Information from Federal Departments and Agencies: Hearings before a Special Subcommittee on Government Operations*, 84th Cong., 1st sess., November 7, 1955.

24. 88 Stat. 250 (1966).

25. S.Rep. No. 813, 89th Cong., 1st sess.3 (1965).

26. *NLRB v. Robbins Tire & Rubber Co.*, 437 U.S. 214, 242 (1978).

27. S. Rep. No. 813, 89th Cong., 1st sess. 5 (1965).

28. *Richmond Newspapers, Inc. v. Virginia*, 448 U.S. 555, 589 (1980); see also Thomas I. Emerson, "The Affirmative Side of the First Amendment," *Georgia Law Review* 15:795, 805, 828 (Summer 1981); Traciel V. Reid, "An Affirmative First Amendment Access Right," *Communications and the Law* 10:39 (June 1988).

29. Craig R. Ducat and Harold W. Chase, *Constitutional Interpretation*, 4th ed. (St. Paul, Minn.: West Publishing, 1988) 1359.

30. Ducat and Chase, 1377.

31. *Freedom and Equality of Access to Information: A Report to the American Library Association* (Chicago: American Library Association, 1986).

32. *ALA Commission*, xv.

33. *ALA Commission*, xi.

34. *ALA Commission*, 13.

35. *ALA Commission*, 111-112.

36. Office of Management and Budget Circular A-130 (as of December

1991).

37. Exec. Order No. 12,356 3 C.F.R. 166 (1982); NTISSC Directive No.2 (1986); *Computer Security Act of 1987*, Pub.L.No. 100-235, 101 Stat. 1724 (1987).

38. Glenn Dickinson, "The Supreme Court's Narrow Reading of the Public Interest Served by the Freedom of Information Act," *Cincinnati Law Review* 59:191 (1990); Lori L. Vallone, "A Further Step Toward a New Exemption 7 of the Freedom of Information Act: John Doe Agency v. John Doe Corp.," *Creighton Law Review* 24:267 (1990); Christopher Dunn, "Judging Secrets," *Villanova Law Review* 31:471 (1986).

39. Office of Management and Budget, "Management of Federal Information Resources," 50 Fed.Reg. 52,730, and 52,736 (1985).

40. Barbara Hale and Sandra McAninch, "The Plight of U.S. Government Regional Depository Libraries in the 1980s," *Government Publications Review* 16:387 (1989).

41. Hale and McAninch.

42. 44 U.S.C. §3501-3520 (Supp.1986).

43. Executive Order No. 12,356.

44. Dunn, "Judging Secrets."

45. General Services Administration, Federal Equipment Data Center, *Automatic Data Processing Equipment in the U.S. Government* (April 1990).

46. General Services Administration, *Microcomputer Survey Report* (September 1988).

47. Ed Roback, computer analyst for NIST, telephone conversation September 16, 1991.

48. Jerry J. Berman, "The Right to Know: Public Access to Electronic Public Information," *Software Law Journal* 3:491 (1989).

49. Berman, 504.

50. Berman, 505ff.

51. Leo T. Sorokin, "The Computerization of Government Information: Does It Circumvent Public Access Under the Freedom of Information Act and the Depository Library Program?" *Columbia Journal of Law and Social Problems* 24:267 (1990).

52. The Freedom of Information Reform Act of 1986, 100 Stat. 3207, at §1801 (codified at 5 U.S.C. §552(a)(4)(A)).

53. James Popkin, "Running the New 'Improved' FOIA Obstacle Course," *Columbia Journalism Review* July/August 1989, 45.

54. Bruce Morton, "The Depository Library System: A Costly Anachronism," *Library Journal*, Sept.15, 1987, 52; J. Timothy Sprehe, "Government Information Policy: Perspectives on Federal Issues," *Bulletin of the American Society for Information Science*, October/November 1991, 9; Ridley Kessler, "Depository Program Expenses for Libraries and Users" (white paper), American Library Association Annual Conference, Atlanta, Georgia, June 1991.

55. Kessler, 8.

56. "GPO/2001: Vision for a New Millennium," U.S. Government Printing Office, Dec. 1991.

Chapter 2

Definitions of 'Information'

INTRODUCTION

For more than a decade the U.S. federal government has been reported to be the single largest consumer and distributor of information in the world.[1] Management of all that information is under the jurisdiction of dozens of agencies in a variety of government branches.[2] Consequently, the definition and management regulations of information have evolved in response to the needs of particular offices or agencies, rather than through a single conceptual understanding or within consistent guidelines.[3]

As this country approaches the 21st century and what has been called an information age,[4] a clear and precise understanding of the concept 'information' is paramount to writing effective and coherent legislation. A survey, however, of the ways in which the word 'information' is used in the federal statutes draws into sharp relief the variety of understandings of that concept.

The search for such a clear and precise understanding of information might naturally turn to an academic discipline called "information science." The legal scholar, however, who is looking for an easy conclusion from information scientists may be disappointed. Information science departments can be found in many highly respected universities throughout the United States.[5] But the parameters of the discipline calling itself 'information science' are yet to be universally accepted, and part of the continuing discussion centers on the definition of 'information.'[6]

Information scientists offer a host of definitions—all of which may be in part useful and accurate—but are certainly not conclusive. The following review across disciplines will first survey the variety of definitions of 'information' in common use, and then those more technical definitions suggested by information scientists. Finally, a comparison is made between these kinds of definitions and the definitions found in some of federal statutes, in order to suggest the usefulness of information scientists' definitions for future legislation.

'INFORMATION'

The word 'information' has a long history in the English language. The *Oxford English Dictionary* traces it to a Latin root, informare (to inform, in the scholastic sense),[7] and cites literary references dating as early as the time of Chaucer.[8] The definitions range among (1) The action of informing; formation or molding of the mind or character, training, instruction, teach; communication of instructive knowledge. (2) The action of informing; communication of the knowledge or news of some fact or occurrence; the action of telling or fact of being told of something. (3) Knowledge communicated concerning some particular fact, subject, or event; intelligence, news. (4) The action of informing against, charging, or accusing.[9]

Many academic disciplines use the term 'information' in a specific way that relates to the needs of each particular discipline. Fritz Machlup provided a short list of these varying definitions in "Semantic Quirks in Studies of Information."[10] For instance, he says, in linguistics 'information' might be said to define word meaning or content.[11] In logic or philosophy, it might refer to exclusive statements.[12] Genetic engineers use the word to describe the messages encoded by nucleotide bases.[13] And in cybernetics, the word 'information' may refer to activity in which there is no human interaction at all.[14]

But as information science[15] began to emerge as a discipline[16] scholars turned to those few who had examined the word 'information' during the 19th century. These are summarized by Marc DeMey[17] who suggests that the term relates specifically to biological systems.[18] Vannevar Bush, however, in his 1945 dicta for the future of information science, directed the science community's attention and conceptualization of information toward the man-made machine that could free man's mind from memory tasks of information storage and retrieval.[19]

Among the more recent scholarship on the definition of 'information' are works by Gordon Miller and L. David Ritchie. Miller notes that there are a multitude of meanings, "both in ordinary usage and in scholarly discourse."[20] He later asserts that the concept of information includes process as well as form with the "deepest etymological and philosophical roots of the concept . . . nourished by the Pythagorean emphasis on form and the Heraclitean emphasis on process."[21]

Miller traces the concept by starting with uses by both Plato and Aristotle. Plato's theory of forms and the possibility of attaining true knowledge of the world through stable, permanent and independently existing forms, ideas or universals (to in-form) is contrasted with Aristotle's theory of forms posited primarily as essential particulars discovered through a series of questions about a thing's responsible factors—material, efficient, final and formal types.

These concepts were subsequently Christianized by Augustine and Thomas Aquinas during the Middle Ages. The essential difference among the concept elements remains one of process and form. During this period, however, the concept elements focused on "the sense that the locus of the information is not primarily (a process—in-forming) within the person informed, but rather in the thing (or substance) communicated—the message or subject matter."[22] Information was, then, instruction that molded.

Miller suggests that with the advance of modern science methods and the thrust toward quantifying, the concept of information changed to one of process rather than instruction that molded. And the outcome in modern language is that

> both machine and human 'information processing' are apparently often envisioned in somewhat of a factory metaphor, in that pieces of raw data are thought to be taken in by the mechanical or human 'factory' and processed into some sort of finished product, such as lists, reports and analyses for machines, and percepts, concepts, and memories for humans.[23]

Miller concludes that the long-time dissociation of information and in-formation makes the reassociation problematic for information scientists. But his thorough analysis of the concept strengthens clear thinking about the use of the term in subsequent analysis of information science literature.

Ritchie's work surveys the literature of the communication discipline, and succinctly describes the variety of uses for the word 'information' there.[24] He found that 'information' includes data, knowledge, and opinion,[25] and that some scholars suggest that it may be thought of as a means of ordering, planning and controlling action.[26] He generalizes, however, that communication scientists "tend to identify information as those aspects of a message that tell something, answer questions, inform someone about something," and that it is "always relevant to the context of some human activity."[27] In conclusion, Ritchie suggests that "information has to do with the way an act of communication (i.e., a message) tells something or informs someone of something: The concept of information is embedded in the concept of communication."[28]

MODERN DESCRIPTIONS WITHIN THE DISCIPLINE OF INFORMATION SCIENCE

A further look at the range of recent scholarly work attempting to define 'information' and 'information science' might be useful at this point in an effort to sort through the most exhaustive and to-the-point research on the concept. The following summaries are grouped into specific contributions to the evolutionary meaning of the term 'information.' The articles cited are found among information science scholarly journals and are not all-inclusive, but rather representative. The groupings are designed to present a pattern for future categorization.[29] The groupings include those works concerned with (a) the definition of the term 'information' exclusively; (b) the definition of the term relative to a specific science field, and (c) the definition of the term as it seems to be assumed, and where the focus of the work is, instead, on some aspect of the field of information science.

EXPLORATION OF EXCLUSIVE DEFINITION

Eugene Garfield[30] makes a useful distinction between an "information society" and an "information-conscious society":

> An 'information society' will be a society in which we take for granted the role of information as it pervades and dominates the activities of government, business and everyday life. The

information society will be characterized by the fact that the
rapid and convenient delivery of needed information is the
ordinary state of affairs.[31]

He goes on to say that while he believes society as a whole is
information conscious, it is not information literate. "An 'information
literate' is a person who knows the techniques and skills for using
information tools in molding situations to problems."[32] Garfield's
separation of terms provides a beginning point for information
scientists' role in society. Information, Garfield suggests, is pervasive
and relates specifically to solving problems.

Soon after Garfield's work was published, Bertram C. Brookes
presented an exhaustive examination of the term 'information.'[33]
Brookes suggests that information is not just sense-data, which would
be purely subjective, but rather adjusts the structure of knowledge,
which is objective and accretive. He goes on to say that information in
isolation is not knowledge; context is part of the equation and part of
the measurement necessary in science.[34] Brookes tries to provide a
philosophical base for information science by using Popperian[35] ontol-
ogy to devise an equation for measurement of the relation between
information and knowledge.[36]

Christopher J. Fox suggested that the common notion of information is adequate for the description of the discipline and supports the
view by a lengthy discussion of terms through philosophy of language
research methods.[37] While including a selection of information
scientists' definitions as a counterpoint,[38] he examines the use of the
term in common language. Though wedded to words like 'knowledge,'
'truth' and 'belief, he insists that 'information' connotes a unique
entity even in common language use, and that perhaps information
scientists could move forward from this point comfortably.

Anthony Debons concisely posits, in an introductory chapter to a
text on the discipline, an array of discrete definitions for terms in and
around information science.[39] Data is defined as letters, numerals,
lines, graphs and symbols, used to represent events and their states,
organized according to formal rules and conventions. Information is
the cognitive state of awareness (as being informed) given representation in physical form (data). This physical representation facilitates
the process of knowing. Knowledge is the cognitive state beyond
awareness, and wisdom implies the application of knowledge as contained in human judgment.[40]

More recently, Michael Buckland suggested that information, in addition to being process and knowledge related, might be thought of as a thing.[41] Buckland divides much of the previous work defining the discipline into two components—process and form—which he describes as having characteristics that are tangible and intangible. Ultimately Buckland takes a much more encompassing view by framing a definition of 'information' in terms of that which is informative.

Subsequently, Tom Stonier defined 'information' in a two part frame.[42] He suggested that (1) information, like matter and energy, is a basic property of the universe; and (2) any system that exhibits organization, contains information.[43] His contention is that information is part of every aspect of the universe. It may be defined in relation to its immediate context but should be recognized as fundamental and pervasive.

This group of information science theorists are defining 'information' in terms of some specific concerns that might be generalized to include content or physical form, and of its relation to knowledge or to action. These concerns include and extend the *Oxford English Dictionary* definition but do not substantially deviate from the common uses described initially by Miller in his history of the word.

The next two sections of the literature review are intended only as a brief survey of the variety of ways that information scientists discuss the concept of 'information.'

RELATIONAL DEFINITION OF 'INFORMATION'

Several information scientists have preferred to describe the term 'information' in ways specific to the needs of the discipline, as they see it. In an early text used by information scientists, Becker and Hayes[44] briefly declare that "information is the basic ingredient of decision making. As the situations in which decisions must be made become more complex, the need for information correspondingly increases."[45] While the authors do not fuss over the definition, they are clear that the term needs recognition, as are Manfred Kochen, Nicholas Belkin and Stephen Robertson.

Manfred Kochen, in a 1974 article, recognizes that information science as a discipline is a convergence of several research vantage points.[46] While he strives to unify the discipline by developing a single research paradigm, his approach describes information in terms mutually useful for each of the converging research vantage points. The term's parameters here are useful and specific only to the frame of reference Kochen defines.

Kochen's vantage points include information theory, computer sciences, behavioral sciences and information science theory in the narrow sense.[47] His description of information is, briefly, that "information is not only stored, communicated, and processed. It is utilized for problem solving, for control, and steering. Above all, information represents, and is represented."[48] Clearly, the term 'information' as described by Kochen is relative to the disciplines included by Kochen, and not as a word with a life of its own.

In their 1976 paper,[49] Belkin and Robertson imply that the discipline is a convergence, and the term 'information' common to all the converging aspects of information science is evidence for modern exclusion rather than inclusion in the new discipline. They cite Wersig and Neveling's suggestion that information science developed "not because of a specific phenomenon which always existed before and which now becomes an object of study—but because of a new necessity to study a problem which has completely changed its relevance for society."[50]

These authors are meant only as examples of the kinds of vantage points that have been taken in defining the discipline not by the terms used by information science practitioners, but rather by the fields relevant to the discipline.

ASSUMED DEFINITION OF 'INFORMATION'

The third grouping includes those information science researchers who assume, either explicitly or implicitly, a definition of the term 'information.' They focus instead on issues or concerns of the field. The following are only examples of ways in which the term is used casually within the range of concerns researched by information scientists.

Victor Rosenberg summarized national information policies and concerns in a 1982 article without thinking there was a need to define information at all.[51] "The need for national policies in the area of information has been made more urgent by new technological developments. . . . It is no longer obvious who is responsible for what."[52] Andrew Aines, also concerned with national information policy, describes the disheartening support and guidance provided by the govern-

ment for information science research without ever defining the field or
denoting the term 'information.'[53]

Rein Turn was concerned about the legal aspects of personal
information when he described and defined protection policies, but
found no need to define the term 'information.'[54] Similarly, Thomas
Surprenant discusses global threats to stored information without
specifically defining information terminology.[55] Robert Chartrand, too,
is concerned about the legal aspects of information technology, but has
no need to define information terms.[56] And as a final example, Barry
Lesser describes information protection issues in a 1988 journal article,
apparently assuming his readers understand his use of the term
'information' implicitly.[57]

DEFINITION OF INFORMATION WITHIN THE FIELD OF LAW

Black's Law Dictionary defines 'information' as "an accusation
exhibited against a person for some criminal offense, without an indict-
ment."[58] This definition relates specifically to legal texts and sub-
stantively is similar to part 4 of the *Oxford English Dictionary* definition cited earlier. An examination of the definitions of 'information'
cited in legislative texts shows that they vary significantly from *Black's
Law Dictionary*.

LEGISLATIVE DEFINITIONS OF 'INFORMATION'

Dozens of federal statutes direct the collection, management and
dissemination of information. Many of these statutes defer the definition of 'information' to another statute. For instance, Title 5's
Authority for Employment[59] and Title 13's Census Administration[60]
laws refer to Title 26's Internal Revenue Code[61] for a definition of
'information.' Similarly, Title 15's Consumer Product Safety[62] law
refers to Title 5's Freedom of Information Act (FOIA)[63] for a definition
of 'information.'

Neither the Internal Revenue Code nor the Freedom of Information Act define 'information' succinctly. Instead, the law defines the
parameters of jurisdiction over information and the kind of information
excluded. These parameters cluster around concerns of content more

often than form and generally ignore both the action of in-forming described in the *Oxford English Dictionary* and the accusatory context
cited in *Black's Law Dictionary* definition.

For example, the National Security chapter of the federal War and
National Defense code defines 'information' as meaning "any information or material, regardless of its physical form or characteristics, that
is owned by, produced by or for, or is under the control of the United
States Government."[64] And the Internal Revenue Code defines
'information' only in terms of what is exempt from public disclosure.
In this case, 'information' may refer to almost any of the conceptual
frames described by information scientists. The legislative language
here fails to succinctly define 'information,' and instead describes what
is not public information, or which information is exempt from public
disclosure. These parameters can be, on their face, very far-reaching
exemptions. For example, "qualified confidential information" is any
information which is subject to the non-disclosure provision of any
local law of the beneficiary[65] or that which it is determined would
seriously impair assessment, collection, or enforcement under the
Internal Revenue laws.[66]

The implied definition of 'information' cited in the Freedom of
Information Act, as another example, applies only to the specific needs
of the law, and not to a more general concept of information. Information is again described in its relation only to what is public and what is
not, rather than what constitutes information. Public information is
described as "descriptions of its [agency's] central and field organization; . . . statements of general course and method; . . . rules of
procedure; . . . final opinions; . . . statements of policy; . . . administrative manuals and instructions."[67] Non-public information is described
as that information that is "specifically authorized under . . . Executive
order to be kept secret in the interest of national defense or foreign
policy; . . . related solely to the internal personnel rules and practices of
an agency; . . . trade secrets; . . . inter-agency or intra-agency
memorandums; . . . personnel files; . . . records or information compiled
for law enforcement purposes; . . . financial institutions' reports; . . .
geological and geophysical data."[68]

Among the more recent legislative efforts to support public access
to government information are the Government Printing Office Electronic Information Access Enhancement Act of 1993 and the Electronic
Freedom of Information Improvement Act of 1993. The titles[69] clearly
indicate a focus on information but the definitions, again, are sketchy

at best. The Government Printing Office Electronic Information Access Enhancement Act says only that the term "'federal electronic information' means federal public information stored electronically."[70] And though the Electronic Freedom of Information Improvement Act says that its purpose is to "(1) foster democracy by ensuring access to public information; (2) improve public access to agency records and information,"[71] the definitions section gives attention to the terms 'agency,' 'record,' and 'search' but not to 'information.' A further attempt at sorting through 'information' labels was offered in a bill by Senator Daniel Patrick Moynihan in 1993 and passed by the senate August 25, 1994, "to create a bipartisan commission to recommend ways to strengthen the protection of classified information and eliminate the classification of non-sensitive information."[72] But again, the attention was on the distinction of 'classified' and 'non-sensitive' rather than on 'information.'

CHARACTERISTICS OF LEGISLATIVE DEFINITIONS

Three characteristics of legislative definitions come to light. For instance, the FOIA description of information relates more often to content rather than form—that is, what the information is about, rather than in what way it is carried—such as trade secrets or geological and geophysical data. But within the same FOIA attempt at definition, it is the form of information, such as memoranda—information that is conveyed in x—rather than 'information' simpliciter that is defined. It is also clear that these content descriptions of information do not reflect the definitions relative to process found in either the *Oxford English Dictionary* (the action of . . .) or *Black's Law Dictionary* (an accusation against . . .).

Other examples of this kind of definition of 'information' in terms of content rather than form, and least of all to *Oxford English Dictionary*'s process or action, include the following.

> "Information" means facts obtained or solicited by the use of written report forms, application forms, schedules, questionnaires, or other similar methods calling either for answers to identical questions from ten or more persons other than agencies, instrumentalities, or employees of the United States . . .[73]

The term "energy information" includes (a) all information in whatever form on (i) fuel reserves, exploration, extraction, and energy resources . . . (b) matters relating to energy and fuels. . . .[74]

The term "proprietary information" means (a) information contained in a bid or proposal; (b) cost or pricing data; or (c) any other information submitted to the government by a contractor and designated as proprietary.[75]

These definitions point to a variety of understandings about the nature of information and are obviously inconsistent with any one concept of it. They separately focus either on form or on content. And they also illustrate the differences among legislative definitions of 'information' as well as differences with authoritative dictionaries.

CONCLUSION

The range of concerns and the confusion about the definition of 'information' in federal legislation are most evident in the large body of Freedom of Information Act adjudication,[76] but the legislative confusion is certainly not confined only to the FOIA. The keenness of the frustration in both legislators and those affected by federal law[77] points to the need for consistent parameters around the concept of information.

Information scientists, however, can only offer the beginnings of a consistent conceptual frame. That frame does loosely distinguish between categories—information as form, information as content, information as knowledge-forming and information as action instigation. But even information scientists are not united on the general concept fundamental to their discipline. Federal statutes as written now do describe, subliminally perhaps, some of these frames for defining 'information.' But legislators could begin to define 'information' more clearly and specifically within the particular categories. And certainly even this much clear-sightedness would lessen some of the general confusion in the laws about information.

As a working definition for the work here we might at least describe the information that is the subject of the legal text as either the content of some message, information simpliciter, or as that which informs, 'information,' then evident by the effect or supposed effect of that message conveyed or carried. Let the terms 'content' and 'carrier' serve as shorthand references. This very simplistic division may not speak to the many ways 'information' is used in specialized fields of research, but it does serve the purpose of helping to sort through the legislative work, as already demonstrated in the examples, and as referred to throughout the rest of this book. If it can be agreed then that this division does exist in legislative text, as demonstrated in the examples just cited, then the simple division here provides a frame for beginning the discussion of information control at a federal legislative level.

NOTES

1. Office of Management and Budget, Management of Federal Information Resources, 50 *Fed.Reg.* 52,730, 52,736 (1985). Also see Peter Hernon, "Equity in Public Access to Government Information," *Government Information Quarterly* 10(3):301 (1993).

2. *1990 Annual Report of the National Computer System Security and Privacy Advisory Board*, Dept. of Commerce, March 1991.

3. For example, see 5 U.S.C. 552, 552a, 552b, 701; 11 U.S.C. 1125(a)(1); 13 U.S.C. 9; 15 U.S.C. 796, 2054; 18 U.S.C. 1905; 19 U.S.C. 2155; 20 U.S.C. 1221; 22 U.S.C. 2403; 26 U.S.C. 274; 41 U.S.C. 423 and 50 U.S.C. 823.

4. Ithiel de Sola Pool, *Forecasting the Telephone: A Retrospective Technology Assessment of the Telephone* (Norwood, N.J.: Ablex Publishing, 1983); James Beniger, *The Control Revolution* (Cambridge, Mass: Harvard University Press, 1986).

5. The *Association for Library and Information Science Education* directory lists several dozen universities in the United States with accredited programs of information science.

6. Dorothy B. Lilley and Ronald W. Trice, *A History of Information Science 1945-1985* (N. Y.: Academic Press, 1989) p.3-5. Also see Brent Ruben and Jorge Schement (eds), *Information and Behavior: The Relationships Between Communication and Information*, Vol. 4 (New Brunswick, N.J.: Transaction Publications, 1993).

7. *The Compact Edition of the Oxford English Dictionary*, Vol. 1 (New York: Oxford University Press, 1971) 1432.

8. *Melib.* (1386) p. 904, "Whanne Melibee hadde herd the grete skiles and resons of Dame Prudence, and hire wise informacions and techynges."

9. *The Oxford English Dictionary* cites 319 instances of the word 'information' contained in the definition of other words.

10. Fritz Machlup, *The Study of Information, Interdisciplinary Messages* (New York: John Wiley & Sons, 1983) 641.

11. Machlup, p. 650.

12. Machlup, p. 651.

13. Machlup, p. 654.

14. Machlup, p. 656.

15. Evidence of information science to be considered a distinct discipline can be found as early 1945, as described by Glynn Harmon, "Opinion Paper on the Evolution of Information Science," *Journal of American Society for Information Science*, 22(4) 1971, 235. The primary contributions at this time came from Vannevar Bush's concern for extending human memory in his article, "As We May Think," *Atlantic Monthly*, 176(1):101 (1945), and S.C. Bradford's examination of the characteristics of documentation, which allowed for a transition to and separation of information science, as described by him in *Documentation* (London: Crosby Lockwood & Son, 1948).

16. Dorothy B. Lilley and Ronald W. Trice, *A History of Information Science 1945-1985* (New York: Academic Press, 1989), suggest that the emergence of the field can be traced to four developments. These are (1) a backlog of scientific and technical reports that had stockpiled during World War II, (2) a continuing increase in funds for science research after the war, (3) the development and advancing technology of computerization, and (4) the forcefulness of several leaders in this particular direction. (p. 3).

17. Marc DeMey, *The Cognitive Paradigm* (Dordrecht: D. Reidel, 1982).

18. Manfred Kochen, "Information Science Research: The Search for the Nature of Information," *Journal of the American Society for Information Science* 35(3):195 (1984).

19. Vannevar Bush, "As We May Think," *The Atlantic Monthly*, July 1945, 101-108.

20. Gordon Miller, "The Concept of Information," in *Information and Behavior*, Vol. 2, Brent D. Ruben, ed. (New Brunswick, N.J.: Transaction, 1988) 28.

21. Miller, pp. 32-33.

22. Miller, p. 37.

23. Miller, p. 40.

24. L. David Ritchie, *Information* (Newbury Park, Calif.: Sage Publications, 1991).

25. William Douglas, "Anticipated Interaction and Information Seeking," *Human Communication Research*, 12:243-258 (1985).

26. James R. Beniger, *The Control Revolution: Technological and Economic Origins of the Information Society* (Cambridge, Mass.: Harvard University Press, 1986).

27. Ritchie, p. 4.

28. Ritchie, p. 61.

29. For a more detailed categorization, see Nicholas J. Belkin, "Information Concepts for Information Science," *Journal of Documentation*, 34:55 (March 1978).

30. Eugene Garfield, "2001: An Information Society?" *Journal of Information Science* 1:209-215 (1979).

31. Garfield, p. 209.

32. Garfield, p. 210.

33. Bertram C. Brookes, "The Foundations of Information Science," *Journal of Information Science* 2:125-133 (1980).

34. Brookes, "Part IV. Information Science: The Changing Paradigm," *Journal of Information Science* 3:11 (1981).

35. Karl R. Popper, *Objective Knowledge: An Evolutionary Approach* (Oxford: Clarendon Press, 1972).

36. Brookes, "The Foundations of Information Science," 131.

37. Christopher John Fox, *Information and Misinformation: An Investigation of the Notions of Information, Misinformation, Informing and Misinforming* (Westport, Conn.: Greenwood Press, 1983).

38. Fox, pp. 40-74.

39. Anthony Debons, Esther Horne and Scott Cronenweth, *Information Science: An Integrated View* (Boston: G.K.Hall, 1988).

40. Debons, p. 8.

41. Michael K. Buckland, "Information as Thing," *Journal of the American Society for Information Science* 42(5):351-360 (1991).

42. Tom Stonier, "Toward a New Theory of Information," *Journal of Information Science* 17:257 (1991).

43. Stonier, p. 258.

44. Joseph Becker and Robert M. Hayes, *Information Storage and Retrieval: Tools, Elements, Theories* (N.Y.: John Wiley & Sons, 1963).

45. Becker and Hayes, p. 3.

46. Manfred Kochen, "Views on the Foundations of Information Science," *Information Science: Search for Identity* (N.Y.: Marcel Dekker, 1974) 174.

47. Kochen, p. 174.

48. Kochen, p. 171.

49. Nicholas J. Belkin and Stephen E. Robertson, "Information Science and the Phenomenon of Information," *Journal of the American Society for Information Science* 27(4):197-204 (1976).

50. Wersig and Neveling as cited by Belkin, p. 197.

51. Victor Rosenberg, "National Information Policies," *Annual Review of Information Science and Technology*, Vol. 17, Knowledge Industry Publications (1982).

52. Rosenberg, p. 4.

53. Andrew A. Aines, "A Visit to the Wasteland of Federal Scientific and Technical Information Policy," *Journal of the American Society for Information Science* 35(3):179-184 (1984).

54. Rein Turn, "Privacy Protection," *Annual Review of Information Science and Technology*, 20:27 (1985).

55. Thomas T. Surprenant, "Global Threats to Information," *Annual Review of Information Science and Technology*, 20:2 (1985).

56. Robert Lee Chartrand, "Information Technology in the Legislative

Process: 1976-1985," *Annual Review of Information Science and Technology*, 21:203 (1986).

57. Barry Lesser, "Information Protection Issues in the Information Economy," *Bulletin of the American Society for Information Science* February/March (1988) 21-22.

58. *Black's Law Dictionary*, abridged 5th ed. (St. Paul, Minn: West Publishing Co., 1983) 398.

59. 5 U.S.C. §3111(D) (1991).

60. 13 U.S.C. §91 (1991).

61. 26 U.S.C. §6103 (b) (1991).

62. 15 U.S.C. §2055 (1991).

63. 5 U.S.C. §552 (1991).

64. 50 U.S.C. 401, Ch. 15 Sec. 6.1(b) "Information" (1993).

65. 26 U.S.C. §274(II)(iii) (1991).

66. 26 U.S.C. §6103(2) (1991).

67. 5 U.S.C. 552(a) (1991).

68. 5 U.S.C. 552(b)(1-9) (1991).

69. Government Printing Office Electronic Information Access Enhancement Act of 1993, S. 564, 103d Cong., 1st sess., Pub.L.No. 103-40 (1993); Electronic Freedom of Information Improvement Act of 1994, S. 1782 and H.R. 4917, 103d Cong., 2st sess. (1994).

70. S. 564, §4104.

71. S.1782, Sec.2(b).

72. "Protection and Reduction of Government Secrecy Act," S.167, 103d Congress, 1st Sess. (1993).

73. 44 U.S.C. §3502 (1991).

74. 15 U.S.C. §796(e) (1991).

75. 41 U.S.C. §423(p)(6) (1991).

76. See, for example, U.S. Justice Department, *Freedom of Information Case List* September 1993.

77. *Freedom of Information Case List 1991* (Government Printing Office, 1992) pp. 667-699.

Chapter 3

The Foreign Agents Registration Act

INTRODUCTION

Following the *Meese v. Keene*[1] adjudication of the mid-1980s, both houses of the U.S. Congress suggested and debated changes to the Foreign Agents Registration Act of 1938 (FARA).[2] Members of the Senate and the House of Representatives sponsored bills amending the FARA[3] repeatedly during several congressional sessions, but none of the amendments successfully moved from the Congress to the President.

In the 1980s legislators wanted to narrow the definitions of "agent for a foreign principal"[4] and "propaganda"[5] contained in the FARA's statutory language. But by the 1990s legislators wanted, instead, to expand the application of the statute so that it would require former U.S. government staff members who lobby for foreign companies doing business in the United States to register more promptly and more fully as "foreign agents." The debates in the 1980s stressed the nature of pejorative definitions, but by the early 1990s the debates evaluated the ethics of U.S. nationals acting as lobbyists for foreign interests. In the 1980s legislators decried executive branch judgment in the selective application of FARA, but by the 1990s that concern faded from the debates as economic concerns, instead, took center stage.

The congressional concerns about the FARA during this period can be divided into concerns about (1) the content of the message carried or provided by agents of a foreign government or interest, and (2) the agent (simpliciter), carrier or conduit of the message. When the FARA was enacted fifty years ago those two general concerns were equally represented in the language of the statute. But fifty years after the FARA's enactment, technology and issue sensitivity about information content and the carrier or conduit of that information have changed significantly. And these two kinds of descriptors for what was once simply referred to as 'information' may now need to be recognized as significantly different. With that recognition it may also be apparent that the FARA, as written fifty years ago, does not easily manage both concerns within the single piece of legislation.

In the course of describing the congressional committee hearings on the FARA, evidence will emerge to suggest that there has, in fact, been a shift in the legislative concerns. These concerns have moved away from information about political overthrow—the content so feared and discussed in the 1930s and 1940s FARA debates—and toward the 1990s concerns about economic distress thought to be caused by government insiders who represent foreign interests. While the thrust of the FARA continues to focus "the spotlight of pitiless publicity"[6] on those who would represent foreign interests within the United States, the information feared is no longer about political overthrow by those outside the government, but rather about a kind of economic overthrow that causes economic distress. This economic distress, the critics claim, is the result of those who used to work within the government helping those who want the United States to lose the "trade war."[7]

The resulting shift in the focus of congressional concerns from strictly political enemies to economic enemies has diverted congressional attention from some of the earlier charges of executive branch abuse of the FARA that were the center of the 1980s debates. And while free expression and a well-informed citizenry are still concerns of the legislative debates about the FARA, there is less speculation about executive branch abuses and more about foreign influences in the United States. In the 1980s Congress seemed concerned about executive branch over-zealousness in applying the FARA, but it appears that by 1992 legislative concerns had turned to other matters.

The following chapter briefly describes the fifty-year history of the Foreign Agents Registration Act. After this overview, a more detailed description follows of the congressional committee debates reconsidering the FARA during the years after the *Meese v. Keene* decision in which the court did not find "propaganda" as defined in the statute's language to be pejorative. Since the heart of the FARA is to monitor "propaganda" sent into the United States by foreign principals or "agents" and that is in turn presented by "information service employees," a review of congressional hearings to amend the FARA will also provide an opportunity to examine the congressional concept of 'information' in terms of its being content-centered or carrier-centered, as discussed in Chapter 2.

A BRIEF HISTORY OF THE FOREIGN AGENTS REGISTRATION ACT

The Foreign Agents Registration Act of 1938 was the result of lengthy investigations by a special House of Representatives committee chaired by John W. McCormack, Democrat of Massachusetts.[8] The committee's charge was to study the post-Depression rise of propaganda sponsored by European fascist and communist governments circulating in the United States.[9] The committee found "incontrovertible evidence . . . to prove that there are many persons in the United States representing foreign governments or foreign political groups, who are supplied . . . with funds and other material to foster un-American activities and to influence the external and internal policies of this country."[10]

The Foreign Agents Registration Act was written, the report continued, with the purpose of requiring all persons who are in the United States for political propaganda purposes—propaganda aimed toward establishing in the United States a foreign system of government, or group action of a nature foreign to the existing institutions of government, or for any other purpose of a political propaganda nature—to register and supply information about their political propaganda activities, their employers, and the terms of their contracts.[11] The FARA's policy and purpose have remained essentially the same since the declarative amendment was added just days after the bombing of Pearl Harbor in 1942.

> To protect the national defense, internal security and foreign relations of the United States by requiring public disclosure by persons engaging in propaganda activities and other activities for or on behalf of foreign governments, foreign political parties and other foreign principals so that the Government and the people of the United States may be informed of the identity of such persons and may appraise their statements and actions in the light of their associations and activities.[12]

A 1943 case, *Viereck v. United States*, gave the Supreme Court an opportunity to examine the FARA. In the resulting court opinion two significant interpretations of the law were made. The first was by Chief Justice Harlan Stone, who wrote that "the general purpose of the legislation was to identify agents of foreign principals who might engage in subversive acts or in spreading foreign propaganda."[13] In the same case, Justice Hugo Black wrote that the FARA rests on "the fundamental constitutional principle that our people, adequately informed, may be trusted to distinguish between the true and the false." Black also wrote that the intention of FARA's labelling requirement is that "hearers and readers may not be deceived by the belief that the information comes from a disinterested source."[14]

1939-1962

The FARA was amended several times between enactment in 1938 and World War II, effectively extending rather than limiting its scope.[15] In 1939 the term "agent of a foreign principal" was expanded to include any person who receives compensation from or is under the direction of a foreign principal.[16] The definition of "foreign principal" was broadened to include domestic organizations subsidized directly or indirectly, in whole or in part, by a foreign country or its agents.[17]

Changes were also made in 1942, just weeks after the United States entered World War II, that included the policy and purpose statement cited earlier. Congress also wanted to add the provision that all material distributed by an agent of a foreign principal must be labeled "political propaganda" and carry the agent's name. President Franklin Roosevelt initially vetoed the amendment[18] because he feared it would interfere with the allied effort of World War II against a common enemy.[19] Specifically he feared the rancor it might cause with the USSR, a World War II ally but under a communist government.[20] The bill was amended to include some exemptions from the FARA registration that included "any person, whose foreign principal is a government of a foreign country the defense of which the President deems vital to the defense of the United States."[21] Additional changes that year included a shift in the administration of the FARA out of the Secretary of State's office and into the Attorney General's office.[22] Registrants were then required to report to the Justice Department, and eventually to the Criminal Division of that arm of the executive branch.

The FARA remained unchallenged and essentially unchanged through the 1950s and the cold war. But as the nation drew closer to significant involvement in Vietnam, and as U.S. sentiment against that involvement grew louder, the Senate Committee on Foreign Relations began hearings in 1962 to study "all nondiplomatic activities of representatives of foreign governments, and the extent to which such representatives attempt to influence the policies of the United States and affect the national interest."[23]

1962-1983

The Senate Foreign Relations Committee chaired by J. William Fulbright, Democrat of Arkansas, received a report compiled in 1962 describing the enforcement problems with the FARA.[24] The committee, which included as members Hubert H. Humphrey of Minnesota, Mike Mansfield of Montana, and Albert Gore of Tennessee, discovered that enforcement had been spotty. During the first six years, 1939-1944, there were 19 indictments, 18 of which resulted in convictions. Most of the convictions were against individuals for failing to register at all, but some were against professional news writers who failed to disclose some facts about their activities for a foreign government or their partial support from a foreign principal.[25] During the next ten years, 1945-1955, two indictments were brought but both suits were eventually dropped, one for lack of evidence and the other after the indicted group filed the necessary registration information. From 1956 to 1962 there were nine indictments, all for failure to file. The report cautioned, however, that "failure to prosecute does not necessarily reflect full compliance with the law. On the contrary, study of the foreign agent registration statements accepted as complete by the Justice Department and placed in their public files, discloses a number of apparent omissions and/or evasions."[26]

The report made a very strong closing statement about the enforcement and usefulness of the FARA. It suggested that enforcement was lax and nearly useless under the existing system of administration. It also suggested that the FARA was little known to the State Department officials who could have been using the compiled files as a means of evaluating that material offered as unsolicited background information about foreign affairs.

> If the act has failed to keep the public informed on foreign
> activities of this type, its administration and enforcement have
> not kept the State Department informed in the same area.
> There is little more than minimal cooperation between these
> two Government agencies with regard to the FARA. . . . The
> result of this lack of coordination is that State Department offi-
> cials closely involved . . . have little knowledge of the work and
> identity of individuals or firms representing various countries.
> Some are not even aware of the act.[27]

The resulting 1966 amendments to the FARA strengthened enforcement measures by adding time limits for registration[28] and stiffer
penalties for non-compliance.[29] There was also an additional statement
of purpose: "The pitiless spotlight of publicity which Congressman
Emanuel Celler so aptly referred to as the purpose of this [FARA] legislation a quarter of a century ago remains its purpose today."[30] The shift
in focus from content to carrier reported by a new statement of purpose
reflects the committee's findings that "the place of the old foreign agent
has been taken by the lawyer lobbyist and public relations counsel
whose object is not to subvert or overthrow the United States Government, but to influence policies to the satisfaction of a particular
client."[31] This shift was toward emphasizing the need to protect "the
integrity of the decision-making process of our Government and the
public's right to know the source of the foreign propaganda to which
they are subjected."[32] And the Justice Department was instructed to
"reassess its administration of the act" and locate responsibility for
administration in the department's Criminal Division.[33]

During these debates, a new concern surfaced over the term
"propaganda" but the 1942 definition remained intact. The concerns
were given action, instead, by adding to the exemptions for compliance
allowed by the Attorney General.[34] Exemptions were also allowed for
attorneys; those soliciting funds and contributions for medical aid, food
or clothing; and those engaged in private and non-political activities.[35]
As observed in a law journal article, "Whether clothed with the respec-
tability of the term 'public relations' or referred to in such sinister
terms as 'political warfare' or 'psychological warfare,' propaganda is a
tool for molding opinion and promoting specific action. The control of
this tool in the hands of foreign interests is the object of the Act
[FARA]."[36]

Much of the interpretation, then, of the specific administration
and requirements of the law was left in the hands of the executive

branch, in spite of some concerns about the appropriateness of that branch's actions during the twenty-five-year history of the FARA. It is interesting, too, that Senator Fulbright would later oppose the Vietnam War and to state, "It is only when the Congress fails to challenge the Executive, when the opposition fails to oppose . . . that the campuses and streets and public squares of America are likely to become the forums of a direct and disorderly democracy."[37]

In 1977, concern about the administration of the FARA resulted in new reports compiled for the Senate Foreign Relations Committee. The committee still included Hubert Humphrey, but also had as members George McGovern of South Dakota, John Glenn of Ohio, Jacob Javits of New York, Charles Percy of Illinois and Howard Baker, Jr., of Tennessee. And the tenor of the initial report was very different from that of earlier reports. "The use of foreign agents to influence governmental policies and programs is neither new or necessarily evil, and by no means, the monopoly of sinister governments."[38] The report continues:

> It is hardly surprising that foreign agents in increasing numbers have been appearing in and around the Nation's capital since the end of the World War II. The United States came out of the war a military and economic colossus. The size and diversity of its economy has an enormous impact upon the economic well-being of other nationals throughout the world.[39]

In light of the changed world situation since the original enactment of the FARA, the report goes on to suggest that "the changes in focus . . . can be significantly advanced by simple language changes within the law to eliminate pejorative connotations."[40] The report suggests the title of the law be changed, for instance, to the Federal Regulation of Foreign Lobbying and Propaganda Act. Apparently, the changing focus Congress now was concerned about was language connotation rather than strict enforcement against foreign influence. Though enforcement was reported as random and ineffective,[41] the problem of compliance was blamed largely on the inferences drawn from the language of the law.[42]

At this point there seemed to be a clear split developing between the intentions of the executive branch and those of the legislative branch. The Justice and State Departments complained only about lack of personnel to manage enforcement, but they made no complaints about the selectivity of that enforcement. The legislative branch, on the other hand, seems to have shifted from a stance that protects citizens and the nation from foreign influences to one that promotes and assists an informed public (as well as the legislators) by attracting wide compliance with a much less threatening law.

The Justice and State Departments wanted to continue to base their judgment of enforcement on the content of the material.[43] There were seven categories of exemptions to the FARA, but all seven were open to wide interpretation by the Justice and State Departments and the burden of proof rested with the person claiming exemption.[44] But Congress wanted to bolster enforcement solely on the basis of the relationship of an individual who is a conduit or carrier of information and the foreign principal or government represented.[45]

The split in emphasis of enforcement of the law versus compliance with the law is evidently shaped by the focuses of the executive branch and the legislative branch. The split seems to have developed along the universal fault lines of the definition of information—content versus conduit or carrier. This split widened during the next decade, but no significant action was taken by the legislature after the 1977 report.

MEESE V. KEENE

In 1983 a renewed interest in the FARA surfaced when the Justice Department labeled three Canadian films as political propaganda under the provisions of FARA. "In this case, the subject of the films and the timing of the department's decision raised serious doubts about the motives of the administration and the use of Foreign Agents Registration Act to chill debate on some of the most important political issues of this decade," said Rep. Don Edwards of California in an opening statement during a committee hearing.[46] These particular films were about acid rain and nuclear disaster.

Representative Edwards went on to suggest, "It may be the fault lies with the statute and its unnecessarily vague and broad definitions. According to one Department spokesman, 'a film about a country that boasts good seaports and low taxes' constitutes propaganda." During the hearings a Justice Department representative, D. Lowell Jensen, reported that the FARA film reviewers applied an objective test to those films they chose to inspect. "This test, in two words, is 'political advocacy.'"[47]

The three films in this particular case were from the National Film Board of Canada (NFBC). The titles were *If You Love This*

Planet, which won an Academy Award for best documentary depicting life after a nuclear war and *Acid Rain: Requiem for Recovery* and *Acid from Heaven*. The Justice Department informed the NFBC that the films were within the statutory definition of "political propaganda"[48] and they would need to place an informational label prominently near the title of the films with an advisory to viewers that the films were issued by a foreign government.[49] The NFBC was also instructed to file dissemination reports with the Justice Department identifying all theaters and other users of the film within the United States. Canada had exported, and submitted to FARA reviewers, about 400 films since 1947. Only one other Canadian film in all those years had been found to be "political propaganda."[50]

The process, as reported by Jensen, involved in this particular case, selecting five films from the 62 exported to the United States by the National Film Board of Canada within a six month period ending June 30, 1982. The NFBC was one of 700 registrants under the FARA at that time, and "this selection process necessarily involves some discretion and expertise, primarily a sensitivity to the leading political themes of the day."[51] The label required by the Justice Department is not a warning, Mr. Jensen pointed out, like those required for cigarette packages, rather it is a "truth in packaging" approach.[52]

A legal challenge to the FARA requirements came almost immediately from California state senator Barry Keene. Keene, a member of the California Bar Association, wanted to exhibit the films without the required labeling and registration, and so filed suit to enjoin the Justice Department on free speech grounds. District Court Judge Ramirez decided that the content-sensitive language of the FARA was a significant threat to First Amendment rights,[53] and in a subsequent case the Justice Department was broadly enjoined from "enforcing any portion of the FARA which incorporates the term 'political propaganda' as a term of art."[54] Eventually the Supreme Court would overrule that decision[55] and find for the Justice Department.[56]

During the 1983 committee hearings, Catherine A. Leroy, staff counsel for the committee, asked Justice Department representatives about the selection process for film reviews. In the course of her questions, she discovered that the films for review were routinely selected on the basis of their titles alone. And of the 700 registrants in the early 1980, only about 10 of those registrants lists were surveyed. She concluded her questions with the summary statement that "the mechanism for review and enforcement is so erratic as to be not very effective." She went on to speculate "If a film distributor thinks up a perfectly innocuous title, if the nuclear freeze movie had been labeled, 'How to Bake a Cake,' he [the Justice Department reviewer] might not have reviewed it. . . . Or if the movie had occurred 20 years ago when this was not an issue, a political issue, you [a Justice Department reviewer] might also not have picked it."[57]

1983-1993

Recommendations from the 1983 report resulted in the introduction of several bills to amend the FARA, but few of them succeeded past committee reporting. In 1983 and 1985 a bill proposed striking the "political propaganda" sections from the FARA.[58] Another 1985 bill suggested changing "political propaganda" to "advocacy material," and changing the FARA's title to the Free Trade in Ideas Judiciary Amendments of 1985.[59] All of these proposed changes tried to shift the focus of the FARA enforcement away from discretionary content analysis and toward a focus of simply identifying who was carrying or presenting information, whether from a foreign government or foreign principal, whatever the particular political content might be. The concern then was about identifying the agent or carrier of the information, and not about the content of the agent's message.

In the 1987 congressional session, a new concern arose about former government employees, particularly from the executive branch, who left their government positions to become lobbyists for foreign principals.[60] Sometimes, it was asserted by congressional members, the lobbyists were less than forthcoming about their new affiliations so that foreign principals appeared to be getting endorsement from nonpartisan former-U.S. government staffers and congressional members.[61] One means of controlling this situation which was reviewed by committee hearing[62] was to amend the FARA to include a required disclosure by former officers or employees of the government with a more detailed account of their activities with foreign principals. This amendment would have also required a statement declaring that the former U.S. employee had not disclosed to the foreign principal any confidential U.S. government information.[63] The amendment was reported out of the committee, but not acted upon by Congress that year. In this case, the concern was about both the content of information (i.e., its confidentiality) and identification of the agent or carrier.

By the 1989 hearings for the Free Trade in Ideas bills[64] committee members were outspoken about the lack of responsibility taken by the legislature for substantive action against the executive branch discretionary excesses in the administration of FARA.[65] "The courts are not the singular guardians of the Constitution. The Congress has a special responsibility as well," Rep. Robert Kastenmeier of Wisconsin said in an opening statement.[66] "We live in a world that transcends borders. The sharing of ideas and information across international boundaries is imperative if we are to retain our competitive advantage. . . . America must set a clear and continuing example to the many other countries struggling to open their hearts and minds." Kastenmeier, it is reasonable to infer, was concerned here about the content of the information, and about not blocking access to information no matter what the source. The Foreign Communications Free Trade Act, H.R. 2689, an amendment to the FARA, was unsuccessful in 1989, but was revived with additional hearings in 1990.[67] Again Representative Kastenmeier reminded the committee members of the stigmatizing effect of FARA regulations.[68] He stressed that the three Canadian films cited in 1983 portrayed ideas that were unpopular with the executive branch, and that by stigmatizing, essentially black listing, the films the Justice Department did "an enormous disservice to all Americans who never got to see or discuss this important, inspiring and moving work."[69] Kastenmeier, again, suggested that the government should not be in the position of censoring information—the content of the message, here—but rather identifying as simply as possible the carrier of the message. In the case of H.R. 2689, the amendment would have stricken the words "political propaganda" and would have provided for disclosure only of the country of origin, rather than of a specific person or group, on the material circulated.[70]

During the hearing, however, Mark Richard, Deputy Assistant Attorney General for the Justice Department, questioned the need to strike the words "political propaganda" and urged the committee not to dilute the FARA's disclosure requirements. "The origin of the materials disseminated is not necessarily reflective of the existence of a foreign principal in a position to control the content of the material," he told the committee.[71] He went on to assert that the FARA's function was to identify not only those ideas that had political content contrary to U.S. policy, but also the agents in control of disseminating such ideas. This, he said, was, and ought to remain, the thrust of the Act's administration. Here the executive branch representative sought equal attention to foreign information content and carrier.

First Amendment scholar Frederick Shauer, on the other hand, said during his testimony before the committee hearings that "whatever the virtues of full disclosure and full identification, those virtues are bought at the price of inhibiting the freest circulation of political information and argument."[72] Professor Shauer went on to suggest that foreign speakers do not possess a special deviousness or a special ability to mold American opinion, and that the FARA is "plainly the product of an era in which fear of foreign governments was more important than cooperation with them."[73] Shauer finally suggested an even stronger amendment to the FARA than the bill proposes, by eliminating the required designation of the country of origin.[74]

But the bill remained in Congress, neither passed nor voted down, because other kinds of FARA concerns being voiced in congressional committees overshadowed the concerns of the Free Trade bill. These concerns included lobbying by former U.S. employees on behalf of foreign principals (information carrier), and had been brought to committee attention as early as 1986.[75] Also among the concerns related to the FARA expressed in Congress was that of foreign influence (information content and carrier) in U.S. commerce.[76]

By 1991 committees in both houses were reviewing extensive amendments to the FARA that spoke to concerns of the executive branch administration of the FARA[77] and concerns about the outdated language in the FARA.[78] The Senate subcommittee on oversight of government management held hearings June 20, 1991, and reviewed testimony about the pervasive problems of incomplete and late filings by foreign agents who do register[79] and about the selective pressure by the FARA administrators on those who should be registering and are not.[80] "These problems," according to Peter Levine, who was legal counsel for the subcommittee, "raise serious questions as to how well FARA is serving its intended purpose of identifying the representatives of foreign interests in the United States and disclosing their activities."[81]

Among those testifying that day was Rep. Dan Glickman, a Democrat from Kansas who was sponsoring a FARA amendment bill in the House of Representatives. At the Senate committee hearing he said his concerns were focused only on identifying who the foreign agents were, and not on the content of the material they supplied:

> The world has changed dramatically since the Foreign Agents Registration Act was originally used to disclose Nazi and communist propaganda in the 1930s and 1940s. With the end of

the Cold War, we should be less worried about ideological indoctrination and focus our concern instead on the global economic competition. . . . Foreign corporations and governments spend hundreds of millions of dollars annually to gain access and advantage in the American economy. They employ influential lobbyists, many of whom are well-respected former United States government officials, to make their case in Washington.[82]

Representative Glickman then outlined the eight changes in the FARA his bill[83] would initiate. These included changing the name of the act to the Foreign Interests Representation Act and a test to determine the level of foreign control in foreign owned entity. He also suggested narrowing the number of exemptions so that there would be less discretion about who had to register.[84] The bill also suggested a change in the term, not the definition of, "propaganda" to "advocacy or informational materials." All of the concerns were about strengthening registration or identifying the agent (the information conduit) and neutralizing concern about content of the information carried on behalf of a foreign principal. No action has yet been taken by the full Congress on this bill.

Hearings in the 1991 House of Representatives' subcommittee on administrative law and governmental relations[85] reviewed three amending bills,[86] two of which directly amended the FARA. Representative Glickman's H.R.1725 has already been described and is the longer of the two FARA amending bills introduced to the House. His testimony in the House subcommittee added some rationale to the motivations for the FARA amendments he proposed.

I know some people . . . have suggested wiping all of the lobbying disclosure laws off the books and starting fresh with a single global statute. Unfortunately, I remember the last time we tried that back in the late 1970s. It was the first time every interest group in Washington was united on anything, and it was against such a proposal. So I would encourage you to look at the FARA aspects on their own.[87]

Glickman's statement makes clear that he and the 29 co-sponsors viewed the FARA as a law about enforcing disclosure of the information conduit, an agent of a foreign principal in this case, and not a law about information content. In additional testimony, Rep. Marcy Kaptur of Ohio reported on statistics gathered by the General Accounting

Office (GAO) that supported the information conduit concern. In a 1990 report the GAO identified 775 foreign agents with files maintained by the Justice Department. "We know the actual number is in the thousands," Representative Kaptur said.[88]

H.R.1381 was introduced by Rep. Tim Johnson of South Dakota in March 1991, a month earlier than H.R. 1725. Representative Johnson and 19 co-sponsors suggested clarifying language about the definition of "foreign principal" so that American companies having greater than 50 percent foreign ownership would be included.[89] And Rep. Frank J. Guarini of New Jersey added a supporting statement during the hearings.

> I consider [FARA] a very important item to focus on because it does affect national policy and our national security. In 1938, the FARA was established to counteract Nazi activities in our country. . . . The efforts of foreign interests to influence U.S. policy and politics have grown considerably in the last 20 years. One main problem is that, despite public disclosure demands by the FARA and other statutes, foreign influence continues to be exercised, for the most part in secret.[90]

He went on to say that the bill would improve the reporting and enforcement of the FARA by "ensuring that there is no misinformation or misrepresentation."[91] Again, the concern here is with the reporting system of agent registration (the information conduit) and punishment of those who do not comply, rather than the selectivity of the review process of those disseminated materials (information content) that are subsequently labeled "propaganda" and required to display a label identifying the source.

And finally, Sen. Max Baucus, a Democrat from Montana, introduced a bill to prohibit presidential campaign staff members from engaging in political activities as agents of foreign principals.[92] The bill was referred to the Senate governmental affairs committee in August 1992. In his accompanying statement, Senator Baucus said, "I believe this issue represents one of Washington's biggest scandals."[93] Senator Baucus was, he said, responding to the reports about James Lake, a senior communications adviser to the Bush campaign, who acted as a lobbyist for the Canadian Forest Industries Council, a Canadian brewery and a Japanese auto company.[94] And Senator Baucus' bill not only prohibits senior campaign officials from participating as such agents, but also bans officials of a successful candidate from lobbying for foreign principals for 15 years after the election campaign. "Statutes such as the Foreign Agents Registration Act have mile-wide loopholes that rend them impotent," he told the Senate. Senator Baucus' concern was clearly not with the particular content of the information Mr. Lake might be providing but rather with Lake's relationships to domestic and foreign governments. And yet he attached his bill to the FARA, a statute designed to control information content provided by a foreign controlled conduit.

CONCLUSION

The Foreign Agents Registration Act of 1938 originally was a statute that gave no attention to distinctions between information content and information carriers or conduits in the greater interest of controlling information flow. And yet during the last decade there has been disproportionate attention given to inhibiting information content as the *Meese v. Keene* case worked its way through the courts. This attention focused on the stigmatizing effect of the word "propaganda" as defined in the FARA. And yet more recently, congressional attention to the FARA shifted almost completely to concerns about the information conduit or carrier. This new attention took the form of identification of "agents of a foreign principal" rather than concern with the problematic definition of "propaganda" as that "information that prevails upon, indoctrinates, converts, induces or in any other ways influences the recipient."

Most recently the attention on amending the FARA has turned almost exclusively to the issue of defining "agent."[95] Interestingly, the agents most carefully proscribed against are former members of the U.S. government who have made career changes, so that one might believe that the enemy once seen to be on the outside is now an enemy seen to be within. The language of the amendments assumes the message brought by the carriers or "agents" will influence the public decision-making process.[96] But the difficulty of controlling the message content seems to have dissuaded any pursuit of more controls of that sort, and shifted efforts instead to legislative activity in the FARA arena almost entirely to managing the messenger.

NOTES

1. *Meese v. Keene*, 481 U.S. 465, 95 L.Ed.2d 415, 107 S.Ct. 1862 (1987).

2. 22 U.S.C. §611 (1992).

3. S. 237, 100th Cong., 1st Sess. (1987); S. 1268, 100th Cong. 2d Sess. (1988); H.R. 1767, 101st Cong., 1st Sess. (1989); H.R. 1280, 101st Cong., 1st Sess. (1989); H.R. 2689, 101st Cong., 2d Sess. (1990); S. 3101, 101st Cong., 2d Sess. (1990); H.R. 1725, 102d Cong., 1st Sess. (1991); H.R. 3597, 102d Cong., 1st Sess. (1991); S. 3203, 102d Cong., 1st Sess. (1991); S. 79, 103d Cong., 1st Sess. (1993); S. 90, 103d Cong., 1st Sess. (1993); S. 349, 103d Cong., 1st Sess. (1993); H.R. 248, 103d Cong., 1st Sess. (1993); H.R. 550, 103d Cong., 1st Sess. (1993); H.R. 823, 103d Cong., 1st Sess. (1993); H.R. 1224, 103d Cong., 1st Sess. (1993); H.R. 1225, 103d Cong., 1st Sess. (1993); H.R. 1395, 103d Cong., 1st Sess (1993); H.R. 1593, 103d Cong., 1st Sess. (1993) and H.R. 2834, 103d Cong., 1st Sess. (1993).

4. 22 U.S.C. §611(c).

5. 22 U.S.C. §611(j).

6. H.Rep. No. 1381, 75th Cong., 1st Sess. 2 (1937).

7. *Foreign Influence in the United States: Hearing Before the Senate Comm. on Commerce, Science, and Transportation*, 101st Cong., 2d Sess. (1990).

8. Staff of the Senate Comm. on Foreign Relations, 95th Cong., 1st Sess., The Foreign Agents Registration Act 5 (Comm. Print, August 1977).

9. Staff of the Senate Comm. on Foreign Relations, 87th Cong., 2d Sess., *Nondiplomatic Activities of Representatives of Foreign Governments* 6 (Comm. Print, July 1962). (*Nondiplomatic Activities 1962*)

10. H.Rep. No. 1381, 75th Cong., 1st Sess. 1,2 (1937).

11. H.Rep. No. 1381, also see *Nondiplomatic Activities* 1962.

12. 22 U.S.C. §611.

13. *Viereck v. United States*, 318 U.S. 236, 241 (1943).

14. *Viereck v. U.S.*, 251.

15. *Nondiplomatic Activities 1962*, 7.

16. 22 U.S.C. 611(c)(1).

17. S.Rep. No 902, 76th Cong., 1st Sess. 1 (1939), also see H.Rep. No 711, 76th Cong., 1st Sess. (1939).

18. H.R.Doc.No. 611, 77th Cong., 2d Sess. 2 (1942). See also Brief for Appellant at 26, *Meese v. Keene*, 107 S.Ct. 1862 (1987).

19. Valerie M. Verduce, "*Meese v. Keene*: An Attempt to Keep the First Amendment from Raining on the Congressional Parade," *Southwestern University Law Review* 17:373, 387 (1987).

20. Alex Nagy, "Word Wars at Home: U.S. Response to World War II Propaganda," *Journalism Quarterly* 67:207 (Spring 1990).

21. 22 U.S.C. 613(f).

22. Exec. Order No. 9176, 7 Fed. Reg. 4127 (May 29, 1942).

23. S.Res. 362, 87th Cong., 2d Sess. (July 6, 1962). See also *Nondiplomatic Activities* 1962, v.

24. Staff of Senate Comm. on Foreign Relations, 87th Cong., 2d Sess., *Nondiplomatic Activities of Representatives of Foreign Governments* 10-14 (Comm. Print July 1962).

25. Staff of Senate Comm. on Foreign Relations, 11.

26. Staff of Senate Comm. on Foreign Relations.

27. Staff of Senate Comm. on Foreign Relations, 13-14.

28. 22 U.S.C. 614(a), two copies of circulated material and a statement detailing information as to the places, times and extent of circulation within 48 hours of dissemination must be provided to the Attorney General's office.

29. 22 U.S.C. 618, 5 years imprisonment and/or $10,000 fine and for lesser infractions 6 months imprisonment and/or $5,000. (1966).

30. *Nondiplomatic Activities* 1962, 4-5.

31. S.Rep. No. 143, 89th Cong., 1st Sess. 4 (1965).

32. S.Rep. No. 143, 5.

33. S.Rep. No. 143.

34. S.Rep. No. 143, 23.

35. S.Rep. No. 143, 24-25.

36. Claude-Leonard Davis, *Georgia Journal of International and Comparative Law* 3: 408 (1973), quoted in Staff of Senate Comm. on Foreign Relations, 95th Cong., 1st Sess., *Foreign Agents Registration Act* 3 (Comm. Print, August 1977).

37. Thomas Powers, *The War at Home: Vietnam and the American People, 1964-1968* (New York: Grossman, 1973), p. 117, from the *New York Times*, April 22, 1966.

38. Staff of Senate Comm. on Foreign Relations 1977, 3.

39. Staff of Senate Comm. on Foreign Relations 1977, 4.

40. Staff of Senate Comm. on Foreign Relations 1977, 13.

41. Staff of Senate Comm. on Foreign Relations 1977, 118.

42. Staff of Senate Comm. on Foreign Relations 1977, 13.

43. 22 U.S.C. 613 (f) as reported in Senate Print 1977, 8. "The Act [FARA] gives the Attorney General discretionary authority to exempt—Any person, or employee of such person, whose foreign principal is a government of a foreign country the defense of which the President deems vital to the defense of the United States while such person or employee engages only in activities which are in furtherance of the policies, public interest or national defense both of such government and of the Government of the United States, and are not intended to conflict with any of the domestic or foreign policies of the Government of the United States."

44. *Federal Lobbying Disclosure Laws: Hearings Before the Subcomm. on Oversight of Government Management of the Senate Comm. on Governmental Affairs*, 102d Cong., 1st Sess., 204 (1991).

45. Staff of Senate Comm. on Foreign Relations 1977, 2-3, "Administration of the Act could be significantly enhanced by the cooperation

of other federal departments and agencies which have responsibilities in allied areas. . . . State and Justice [departments], for example, have yet to settle on procedures which might measurably improve administration of the Act. . . . Justice Department materials and recent litigation suggest that exemptions authorized by the Act are being used to cloak covert activities. . . . Despite recent charges of efforts by foreign interests to corrupt the legislative process and similar efforts by agents of the United States and American business to influence foreign political and commercial policies, lobbyists for foreign interests, like their domestic counterparts, can and do serve a 'useful role.'"

46. *Canadian Films and the Foreign Agents Registration Act*, Oversight Hearing Before the Subcomm. on Civil and Constitutional Rights, Comm. on the Judiciary, 98th Cong., 1st Sess. 1 (March 18, 1983) Serial No. 36. (*Canadian Films* 1983)

47. *Canadian Films* 1983, 5.

48. 22 U.S.C. §611(j). "Any oral, visual, graphic, written, pictorial or other communication or expression by any person (1) which is reasonably adapted to, or which the person disseminating the same believes will, or which he intends to, prevail upon, indoctrinate, convert, induce, or in any other way influence a recipient or any section of the public within the United States with reference to the political or public interests, policies, or relations of a government of a foreign country or a foreign political party or with reference to the foreign policies of the United States or promote in the United States racial, religious or social dissensions, or (2) which advocates, advises, instigates, or promotes any racial, social, political, or religious disorder, civil riot, or other conflict involving the use of force or violence in any other American republic or the overthrow of any government or political subdivision of any other American republic by any means involving the use of force or violence."

49. "This material is prepared, edited, issued or circulated by (name and address of registrant) which is registered with the Department of Justice, Washington, D.C., under the Foreign Agents Registration Act as an agent of (name and address of foreign principal). This material is filed with the Department of Justice where the required registration statement is available for public inspection. Registration does not indicate approval of the contents of the material by the United States Government." Directed, §614(b).

50. "Canadian Film Order Sparks Lawsuits, Bill," *News Media & the Law*, Jan./Feb. 1984, p. 8.

51. *Canadian Films* 1983, 13.

52. *Canadian Films* 1983, 15.

53. *Keene v. Smith*, 569 F. Supp. 1513 (1983).

54. *Keene v. Meese*, 619 F. Supp.1111 (E.D.Cal. 1985).

55. *Meese v. Keene*, 481 U.S. 465 (1987).

56. For reaction to the decision from the legal community see Ava Marion Plakins, "Political Propaganda," *Fordham International Law Journal*

11:184 (1987); Rodney A. Smolla and Stephen A. Smith, "Propaganda, Xenophobia, and the First Amendment," *Oregon Law Review* 67:253 (1988); Robert G. Waters, "The Foreign Agents Registration Act: How Open Should the Marketplace of Ideas Be?" *Missouri Law Review* 53:795 (1988).

57. *Canadian Films* 1983, 49.

58. H.R. 1969, 98th Cong. 1st Sess. (1983); H.R. 3957, 99th Cong. 1st Sess. (1985)

59. H.R. 3827, 99th Cong., 1st Sess. (1985).

60. S.Rep. No. 100-101, 100th Cong. 1st Sess. (1987).

61. S.Rep.No. 100-101, 2.

62. See S.237 (1987) and Senate Comm. on the Judiciary meeting May 19, 1987.

63. S.Rep.No. 100-101, 16.

64. Only H.R. 2689, *Foreign Communications Free Trade Act of 1989*, 101st Cong., 1st Sess. (1989), would actually amend FARA.

65. *Free Trade in Ideas: Hearings Before the Subcomm. on Courts, Intellectual Property, and the Administration of Justice*, H.R. Comm. on the Judiciary, 101st Cong., 1st Sess. (May 3 and 4, 1989).

66. *Free Trade in Ideas: Hearings*, 2.

67. *Foreign Communications Free Trade Act of 1989: Hearing Before the Subcomm. on Courts, Intellectual Property and the Administration of Justice*, H.R. Comm. on the Judiciary, 101st Cong., 2d Sess. (March 29, 1990).

68. *Foreign Communications: Hearing*, 5.

69. *Foreign Communications: Hearing*, 5, Kastenmeier quoting Mitchell Block who appeared as a witness in the 1989 hearings.

70. H.R. 2689 §3(a)(2) (1990).

71. *Foreign Communications: Hearing*, 19.

72. *Foreign Communications: Hearing*, 39.

73. *Foreign Communications: Hearing*, 40.

74. *Foreign Communications: Hearing*, 41.

75. S. 2324, 99th Cong. 2d Sess. (1986). See also S.Rep.No. 100-101, 100th Cong., 1st Sess. 2 (1987). "Some former Federal employees were using their access and influence, gained through Government service, for personal financial gain; and some former employees were using sensitive information, vital to national interests, for financial gain by directly or indirectly sharing this information with foreign interests."

76. S. 3101, 101st Cong., 1st Sess. (1990); *Foreign Influence in the United States: Hearing Before the Senate Comm. on Commerce, Science and Transportation*, 101st Cong., 2d Sess. 44 (1990). "Persons engaged in 'political' activities on behalf of foreign-owned U.S. companies would be required to register as foreign agents. . . . Together with the proposed change, political activity would include not only Washington representatives and public affairs officers of foreign-owned U.S. corporations, but also chief executive officers and other senior managers in connection with certain aspects of the

ordinary course of their activities. . . . [It is] estimated that the number of registrants would rise from the current 900 to at least 18,250." (46).

77. *The Federal Lobbying Disclosure Laws: Hearings Before the Subcomm. on Oversight of Government Management of the Senate Comm. on Governmental Affairs*, 102d Cong., 1st Sess. (1991).

78. *Modification of the Foreign Agents Registration Act of 1938: Hearings Before the Subcomm. on Administrative Law and Governmental Relations of the H.R. Comm. on the Judiciary*, 102d Cong., 1st Sess. (1991).

79. *Federal Lobbying Disclosure Laws*, 3.

80. *Federal Lobbying Disclosure Laws*, 4. Also see General Accounting Office Materials, 464-478, and Executive Branch Materials, 479-501.

81. *Federal Lobbying Disclosure Laws*, 164.

82. *Federal Lobbying Disclosure Laws*, 153.

83. H.R. 3597 (1991).

84. *Federal Lobbying Disclosure Laws*, 154.

85. *Modification of the Foreign Agents Registration Act of 1938: Hearings Before the Subcomm. on Administrative Law and Governmental Relations of the H.R. Comm. on the Judiciary*, 102d Cong., 1st Sess. (1991). (*Modification: Hearings*.)

86. H.R. 1725, H.R. 1381 and H.R. 806.

87. *Modification: Hearings*, 29.

88. *Modification: Hearings*, 37.

89. *Modification: Hearings*, 73-74.

90. *Modification: Hearings*, 75.

91. *Modification: Hearings*, 75-76.

92. S.3203, 102d Cong., 2d Sess. (1992).

93. 138 *Congressional Record* S.12663 (daily ed. August 12, 1992).

94. 138 *Congressional Record* S.12663.

95. See, for instance, S.349 (1993), "To provide for the disclosure of lobbying activities to influence the Federal Government, and other purposes."

96. See, for instance, H.R. 823 (1993), "To provide for the disclosure of lobbying activities to influence the Federal Government, and for other purposes," and Sec. 2(1), "responsible representative government requires public awareness of the efforts of paid lobbyists to influence the public decisionmaking process." And then Sec.3, where the only definitions are for "agency," "client" and "covered executive branch official," meaning the President, Vice President, any officer or employee of the Executive Office of the President other than a clerical or secretarial employee, and any officer or employee serving in an Executive level position.

Chapter 4

The Computer Security Act of 1987

INTRODUCTION

A special issue of *The Quill*[1] in 1991 reported on the growing concern among journalists who are encountering increased difficulty obtaining access to federal government-held information stored in computer databases. Though the Freedom of Information Act (FOIA) has proved a useful tool for journalists seeking ways to loosen the executive branch's hold on classified information,[2] journalists are finding that the FOIA does not meet all their computer-age needs.[3]

In both 1991 and 1993 Sen. Patrick J. Leahy introduced bills to amend the FOIA to include computer records.[4] His 1993 Electronic Freedom of Information Improvement Act went so far as to direct that federal agencies provide information in any form in which such records are maintained, and that "reasonable efforts" be made to provide records in an electronic form even when such records are not usually maintained in that form. There are, however, existing entanglements for FOIA's expanding to computer records; one of these is the Computer Security Act of 1987. This chapter examines the Computer Security Act (CSA) as one way that the government may be able to use the law to deny public access to government-held information in the name of national security.[5] As recently as February 1994 at least one senator called for stronger enforcement of the CSA and hearings to examine the possibility of strengthening the act.[6]

The statutory language of the Computer Security Act contains a section disallowing its use as the sole legal grounds for rejection of

FOIA requests.[7] But the law has not been tested by the courts and is not completely implemented yet.[8] The following review of the CSA, however, points to the ways in which the act provides for expanding the kinds of material protected against public access, and thus kept out of the information flow.

Troublesome definitions for 'information' and 'sensitive' were not adequately addressed or universally understood at the time of the congressional hearings for the CSA,[9] and these troublesome definitions remain to plague those charged with administering the CSA.[10] Throughout the hearings for the CSA, congressional leaders and members giving testimony tried to sort out the difficulties with the working definitions, but they were never able to recognize and clarify the confusion over characterizations of 'information' that spoke only to either information content or information carriers—in this case the computer database. This characterization by committee members and the rationale given for their legislating protection for either information content or information carriers are the primary subjects addressed.

BACKGROUND ON FOIA RELEVANT TO THE COMPUTER SECURITY ACT

The Freedom of Information Act[11] provides for public access to government-held documents, both those generated by the government and those processed by the government. The FOIA contains nine exemptions to public access of government documents. These include an exemption for any material classified in the interest of national security (Exemption 1) and an exemption for information specifically described as exempt by federal statute (Exemption 3).

Exemption 1 relies on a classification system established by executive order and includes the categories "top secret," "secret" and "confidential."[12] These classifications are defined in the *Code of Federal Regulations*.[13] Hundreds of complaints have been filed against government agencies applying Exemption 1 status to material held by these agencies, and about 100 federal court cases have been resolved during the past 20 years.[14] Almost half of these cases conjunctively disputed the use of Exemption 3 to reject FOIA requests for federal agency information.[15]

Exemption 3 relies on a two-pronged test that requires (1) that the statutory language cited leave no discretion as to which materials are to be withheld from public scrutiny, or (2) that particular criteria for withholding be described clearly in the language of the statute. In the past 20 years more than 200 federal court cases have been decided in which Exemption 3 was applied by federal agency officials to government-held data.[16] In more than a quarter of these cases agency officials tried to use both Exemption 1 and Exemption 3 to deny FOIA requests.

In a 1990 *American Bar Association Journal* article,[17] Richard L. Fricker reported that nearly half of the FOIA lawsuits pending in U.S. courts had been filed in the first year after President George Bush took office. The administration's obsession with secrecy, he says, is a carry-over from Reagan's eight-year presidency. Concern about FOIA use and abuse increased during those ten years.[18]

EXEMPTION 1

In the most thorough examination of FOIA Exemption 1 history recently published,[19] Christopher Dunn catalogued the historical uses and abuses of the classification system and the judicial response to executive power over state secrets up to and including the implementation of the 1982 directive from the president on classification, Executive Order 12,356. Dunn notes that the current considerations for the court in questions of Exemption 1 application are (1) the classifiability of the information and (2) the ramifications of its unauthorized disclosure.

The assumption by the courts, Dunn explains, is that agencies have carefully prepared criteria for classifying information, and that assumption has led the court to defer to the agency's decision about classifiability. The second consideration—the ramifications of unauthorized disclosure—can and should be made by judges, who, Dunn contends, are just as expert at predicting the future as the executive branch is. If this consideration is left in the hands of judges who need not defer to executive branch members then politically based Exemption 1 decisions could be prevented. Dunn adds, "The contention that the executive branch should have the final say over the political decisions that result in the denial of public access to government documents attributes a degree of trustworthiness to the executive branch that it has demonstrated it does not deserve."[20]

Dunn concludes that courts are increasingly abdicating this checks-and-balance role in favor of deference to the executive branch experts. In support of his conclusions he cites a series of cases leading to the precedent-establishing *EPA v. Mink*,[21] which filtered down to lower court decisions such as *Abbotts v. Nuclear Regulatory Commission*[22] in which the courts held that "courts are required to accord substantial weight to an agency's affidavits concerning the details of the classified status of a disputed record."[23]

EXEMPTION 3

A 1984 examination[24] of the CIA's use of Exemption 3 reported much variation in the judicial application of de novo review process called for in Exemption 3 requests. A case in point is examined by Michael H. Hughes,[25] who describes the Court's decision in *CIA v. Sims*[26] in which the Central Intelligence Agency denied a FOIA request on the grounds of Exemptions 1 and 3.

A 1988 article reviewing FOIA activity[27] cited new statutory regulations that supported Exemption 3 rejection of requests. These recent developments include Section 6103 of the Internal Revenue Code, protecting all tax return information,[28] and The Trade Secrets Act, prohibiting federal employees from releasing trade secret information they receive on the job unless they are legally authorized to do so.[29] This article also noted the Computer Security Act and reported the disclaimer section contained in that law.

EXECUTIVE ORDER 12,356

In 1982 President Reagan issued Executive Order 12,356 directing a unified classification system to safeguard national security information. This was not unusual for a U.S. president.[30] But Reagan's order directed information safeguards at a higher level than any previous administration since the 1950s.[31] President George Bush did not supersede this order with one of his own.

Reagan's order instructed agency officials:

> If there is reasonable doubt about the need to classify information, it shall be safeguarded as if it were classified pending a determination by an original classification authority, . . . If there is reasonable doubt about the appropriate level of classification, it shall be safeguarded at the higher level of classification pending a determination by an original classification authority.[32]

Reagan's order also directed that "information shall be classified as long as required by national security considerations,"[33] thus eliminating the time frames that used to trigger declassification automatically.[34] Moreover, Reagan's order directed that information may be classified or reclassified,[35] even after it has been published in the public domain[36] or after it has been requested under the FOIA.[37]

Still concerned about security measures, President Reagan issued a policy statement in 1984 that cautioned executive branch civilian employees to be particularly careful about computer system data security anywhere they might see questionable users with access, inside or outside the direct executive branch domain. National Security Decision Directive 145,[38] Reagan's written version of the statement, came to Congress' attention only after private computer data companies complained about the government's higher scrutiny of private computer database customers and after the Department of Defense asserted that unclassified information pieced together could be a national security threat.[39]

Assistant Secretary of Defense Donald Latham said in a May 27, 1986, *Washington Post* article, "I'm very concerned about what people are doing, and not just the Soviets. If that means putting a monitor on NEXIS type systems, I'm for it." Mead Data Central, a private commercial company, produces NEXIS for subscribers as a computer database service that includes newspaper, magazine and other public domain material. After Latham's remarks, Jack W. Simpson, president of Mead Data Central, said he started paying very close attention to the issue of executive branch over-zealousness on security matters.[40]

Again, in 1986, a directive dubbed the "Poindexter Directive"[41] because the memo came out over John Poindexter's signature established executive branch guidelines for restriction of access to information that was deemed "sensitive."[42] "Sensitive" was defined in the directive as "information the disclosure, loss, misuse, alteration, or destruction of which could adversely affect national security or other Federal Government interests."[43]

CONGRESSIONAL ACTIVITIES

In 1985 a House subcommittee of the government operations committee heard testimony[44] concerning a proposed bill, the Computer Security Research and Training Act of 1985.[45] The bill was intended to provide for research within the National Bureau of Standards to assess the vulnerability of government computers and communication, the development of technical and management strategies against access to sensitive information, and mandatory training for employees in computer and communication security.[46]

During the hearing considerable concern was expressed about the expansion of the executive branch controlled Department of Defense (DOD) authority under NSDD-145 into non-classified information.[47] While congressional members agreed with the general concern about computer database vulnerability, the "misuse, penetration or manipulation by disgruntled employees, terrorists, or others with criminal intent,"[48] they were not sure that DOD was the appropriate arm for administration of private sector and civilian agencies.[49] There was some attention given to sorting out the content of the information to be protected—"sensitive"—from the carrier of the message—computers. But the ramifications of an all-purpose use of the term "sensitive information" received little attention, while most of the hearing concerned the general division of authority over executive branch and public sector computer, and automated information systems.

Rep. Dan Glickman of Kansas, a sponsor of the bill, suggested that on several counts the Institute of Computer Sciences and Technology within the National Burueau of Standards (NBS) was a better administrative arm for such legislation than the DOD. He suggested that since the NBS was already working on computer standards for civilian agencies and industry they were in a good position to also assess security needs in these areas. And because the Institute of Computer Sciences and Technology was a non-regulatory agency, no laws governing it would be created without explicit action from Congress. The committee agreed with the solutions of H.R. 2889, but the bill did not reach a floor vote.

Instead the bill was amended to The Computer Security Act of 1986[50] in order to address three major issues: concern over computer privacy and security, the impact of NSDD-145 in setting federal civilian computer security, and the role of the federal government in training employees in computer security standards.[51] While the first issue—privacy and security—concerns the actual content of the information protected, the other issues speak more directly to concerns about power and control, or who will administer computer security. Again, Congress is concerned here with protecting citizen access to information against executive branch politics, but the issue of information content has become a muddying factor in review of the proposed law.

On the issue of "sensitive information," a House subcommittee report on the bill said:

> One of the benefits of a full and open society is the rich exchange of ideas and knowledge unfettered by governmental intervention and redtape. . . . Since it is a natural tendency of DOD to classify everything, it would be impossible for the department to strike an objective balance between the need to safeguard information and the need to maintain the free exchange of information.[52]

Clearly, then, congressional intent was to take the power of information control in federal civilian agencies away from the executive branch. But a clear understanding of the word 'information' was rarely addressed, and usually was attached as an adjective to words for computer databases, rather than used separately and independently. The rest of this chapter focuses attention on the specifics of the definition of "sensitive information" that emerged during congressional debate; this issue brings into high relief the possible misapplication of the law where confusion about 'information' exists.

The Computer Security Act of 1987

Congressional committee hearings on computer security measures, which began in February 1987,[53] examined the concerns expressed in Congress about executive branch activity in computer security and national security breaches and those expressed by computer database companies and subscribers of those services about infringements on public domain information.[54] Many groups submitted letters and sent representatives to appear as witnesses against adoption of any law that would impede access to information. The American Society for Information Science (ASIS), for instance, wrote to the committee:

> Proposals to limit access to unclassified economic, scientific and technical data that exist in the databases of the federal government and private companies are an unacceptable violation of fundamental rights. These rights and others are further infringed when limitations are based not on information *content*, but rather on information *form*.[55]

The greatest concern among the database companies was that the

NTISSC Directive No. 2 and the proposed H.R.145 defined the term 'sensitive' in identical language,[56] language which appeared to restrict access to that information designated 'sensitive,' even though presumptively all information outside the executive order classification system is public information—that is, unrestricted.[57]

The language of the House bill was amended slightly to read:

> The term "sensitive information" means any information, the loss, misuse, or unauthorized access to or modification of which could adversely affect the national interest or the conduct of Federal programs, or the privacy to which individuals are entitled under section 552a of title 5 (Privacy Act), but which has not been specifically authorized under criteria established by an Executive order or an Act of Congress to be kept secret in the interest of national defense or foreign policy.[58]

The Act, voted through the House and Senate and signed into law by President Reagan on January 8, 1988, also includes a closing section that directs:

> Nothing in this Act, shall be construed (1) to constitute authority to withhold information sought pursuant to section 552 of title 5; or (2) to authorize any federal agency to limit, restrict, regulate or control the collection, maintenance, disclosure, use, transfer or sale of any information that is (A) privately-owned information; (B) disclosable under section 552 of title 5, or other law requiring or authorizing the public disclosure of information; or (C) public domain information.[59]

This disclaimer does not, however, guard against Executive Orders or further acts of Congress.

The CSA designates the National Bureau of Standards to develop and implement the standards that "improve the security and privacy of sensitive information in federal computer systems."[60] The CSA also designates the establishment of an advisory board that advises and reports to the Secretary of Commerce, the Office of Management and Budget, the National Security Agency and Congress. In that committee's first annual report, the board defined its authority as extending "only to those issues affecting the security and privacy of unclassified information in federal computer systems or those operated by contractors or state and local governments on behalf of the federal government."[61]

The 12-member board, representatives of private industry as well as government agency officials, has met at least three times a year since its charter in May 1988. Recurring was the problem of carefully defining "sensitive information" in terms of some sort of categorization system so that a standard could be applied across the government agencies handling computer database material.

In 1988, the General Accounting Office reported to a House subcommittee on the implementation of the CSA.[62] The report said that 89 federal agencies had received a questionnaire about their compliance with the CSA.[63] Five agencies responded that they were not subject to the act. One of those five was the CIA. But of the remaining 84 agencies, only four did not respond at all, and 74 agencies said they were able to identify all of their sensitive computer systems, in compliance with the CSA definitions.[64]

When the 1989 report was submitted to the House subcommittee, the Commerce Department's National Institute of Standards and Technology (NIST) was still in the process of collecting and evaluating the 1,500 existing security systems and plans provided to them as the result of the previous year's questionnaire.[65] Progress was very slow, according to the report, but Ray Kramer, deputy director of the NIST, told committee members, "I hope that in the 1990s we can say that the Federal government leads the nation in developing and using cost effective security controls."[66]

Other House members were less optimistic about the progress of separating military and civilian computer security issues.[67] Among the administrative directions given the Commerce Department by Congress was one to develop a "memorandum of understanding" with the National Security Agency, an agency of the executive branch. The role of NSA was to be strictly advisory, Rep. John Conyers, chairman of the subcommittee, told members. He reminded the committee that the Computer Security Act was an attempt to "strike a balance between [national security] interests and the interests of the public to protect sensitive personal and financial data."[68] But the understanding reached, he said, "weakens civilian control [that] will upset the balance and will result in unwarranted personal intrusions and inhibitors to both domestic and international commerce—a result all of us clearly want to avoid."[69]

Committee members listened to testimony and received letters from the public about the kinds of intrusions they had experienced at the hands of the National Security Agency, and what they expected from further efforts by NSA. Jerry Berman, director of the American Civil Liberties Union, summed up the civilian concerns about NSA. Berman told the committee, "Military control might well succeed in establishing effective computer security, but at the expense of the free flow of information, the public's right to know, the First Amendment values, including the right of citizens to be free of unwarranted intelligence surveillance."[70] Among the NSA activities Berman cited were instances of the executive branch's reclassifying data already disseminated to private data vendors in order to impede access to the information, and of its threatening commercial database firms with prosecution under the export control laws for failure to limit data dissemination.[71] The result of the hearing was simply a stronger warning to NSA members not to overstep their bounds.[72]

Again the House subcommittee overseeing implementation of the Computer Security Act heard testimony and received reports in 1990.[73] This time Clifford Stoll, an astrophysicist and author of the *The Cuckoo's Egg*,[74] testified before the committee and urged an expanded network of cooperation with enforcement agencies.[75] "Suppose you walked along a city street, trying to force doors open. How long would it take before someone called the cops? Five houses? Ten?" Stoll asked the committee.[76] He suggested that computer security be thought of in terms of more strictly enforced penalties for violation so that those misusing the database would be penalized and deterred from further such activity.[77] But as Stoll spoke, members questioned his concerns about access to unclassified information.

Rep. Tom Campbell of California tried to summarize Stoll's concerns during the hearings. "The question is not so much that our classification safeguards broke down, but that we may not be covering as much as you wish or I wish under the classification [system]," Representative Campbell suggested. Stoll replied, "The concern is that some information, though it's not classified, you do not want someone else to read." Campbell again summarized, "[Computer security is] not so much a system architecture problem as it is a classification problem."[78] Campbell, it seems, was trying to distinguish between the carrier, in this case the computer database, and the content of the message.

In 1991 an advisory committee of the board reported that no consensus of the definition of 'sensitive' could be found among government agencies now using a category of "sensitive unclassified information."[79] The advisory committee reported that the "implementation of a unified,

consistent categorization standard for sensitive unclassified information throughout the government is not realistic," but that "there is a
need for a method to describe the expected handling of information that
is sensitive to disclosure when shared between agencies."[80]

During House subcommittee hearings in 1991, Rep. Don Ritter of
Pennsylvania urged members to look specifically into the problems of
"protecting America's computer and information systems from viruses,
hackers, electronic theft and even potentially hostile foreign
interests."[81] This plea could be likened to a call for concern in many
library board meetings about books that deteriorate from moisture, are
cut apart by those not permitted to check them out, or are stolen to be
sold illegally.

The first witness of the hearing, Winn Schwartau of the International Partnership Against Computer Terrorism, reported to the committee that 50 million computers are interconnected into a global
network, and that "it is impossible to consider the federal computer
systems as isolated entities any longer."[82] He reported, too, on the
number and range of computer crimes that were invisible to law enforcement agencies as the laws stood then.[83] He suggested that the committee consider ways of strengthening computer security by re-
examining the classification policies and standards for information held
in government-controlled computers.[84] And, finally, he urged the committee to define the criteria by which the public actually controls its
data, security and methods of disclosure. "We need to address that in
part and parcel of a national [information] policy. . . . In the further the
Computer Security Act can be expanded to take into consideration
some of these points."[85]

At no point in his testimony did Schwartau explicitly distinguish
between the content of the database and the computer system holding
information, and yet his concerns seemed to be with protecting the
system rather than guarding particular information content. He mentioned viruses, which are indiscriminate about what kind of information content they destroy, and electromagnetic eavesdropping, which is
also indiscriminate about which information it picks up. Both of these
are concerned with breaking into systems, whatever their content. And
yet the focus of the Computer Security Act is on a certain kind of
information—"sensitive information" held in a computer database—not
just any kind of information or computer system.

CONCLUSION

Ed Roback, a computer scientist in the Department of Commerce working with the NIST and Computer Security Act advisory board, said that there are several problems with implementing a standard for "sensitive information." These are, he said, developing a uniform definition for sensitive information and trying to cope with the uncertain legal status of the category among the official classification standards.[86] The application of such an information classification category outside the executive order standards now in place could create further problems for FOIA requests when employees are bound by the CSA.

On the face of the CSA statutory law, "sensitive information" is to be protected on the grounds of national security interests, and yet the law also directs that FOIA requests not be denied on the basis of the CSA alone. The question remains whether the CSA designation of computer databases as the parameter of implementation for information protection is inside or outside the FOIA frame of information concerns. The intent of a certain law and the application of that law have often proved to be different things in U.S. history.[87] Clearly, from the testimony given at the congressional hearings preceding enactment of H.R.145, the concerns about executive branch over-zealous security measures were taken seriously and an attempt at protecting against such activity was intended as part of the final legislation.

Congress intended to curb executive branch control of information security by passing first the Freedom of Information Act and perhaps, to a lesser degree, the Computer Security Act. But the subtle information vacuum feared by librarians and spoken of during the congressional hearings may continue. This information vacuum—data that is never evident to those outside the government because it never even reaches any publicly accessed form—is hard to detect by its very nature. "It's hard to know what's missing unless you know what could or should be there," said Anne Heanue, a member of the American Library Association's Washington, D.C., bureau.[88] She said she has noticed fewer documents released to the public by the Departments of Defense and Energy and NASA. "I don't know why there are fewer documents; if it's just lower output or a curtailing of the flow. Indirectly, it leads me to believe an additional filter is in place, and it could be a sensitive classification, beyond what we used to have."

Some of these problems, however, could be eliminated if there had been more attention given to the concept of information initially, so that the law addressed security measures on the grounds of a carrier or conduit rather than attempting to address the security measures to a newly designated kind of information content. It is, as noted throughout the testimony of CSA hearings, the executive branch which was concerned with denoting a "sensitive information" category by which new restrictions could be administered. Congress, in this case, seemed willing to concede the definition of "sensitive information" in order to secure a particular kind of information conduit—the computer database—that members obviously thought needed immediate security attention.

NOTES

1. Traci Bauer, "Electronic Lock," *The Quill*, Oct. 1991, 23.

2. Senator Daniel Patrick Moynihan introduced a bill, S.167, on January 21, 1993, in which he reported that in 1990 6,797,720 documents were classified. He went on to say, "The burden of managing nearly 7 million newly classified documents every year has led to reduced communication within the government and within the scientific community, reduced communication between the government and the people of the United States, tremendous expense and the selective and unauthorized public disclosure of classified information." §202 (d).

3. See, for example, "FYI Media Alert 1991," The Reporters Committee for Freedom of the Press (Washington, D.C.: FOI Service Center, March 1991).

4. "Electronic Freedom of Information Improvement Act of 1991," S.1940, 102d Congress, 1st Sess. 1991; "Electronic Freedom of Information Improvement Act of 1993," S. 1782, 103d Congress, 1 Sess., Nov. 23, 1993.

5. Pub.L.No. 100-235, 101 Stat. 1724 (1987).

6. "Computer Network Crimes," *Congressional Record*, 140:9, S.946, for February 1, 1994.

7. 101 Stat. 1730.

8. Staff of Subcomm. on Technology and Competitiveness of the H.R. Comm. on Science, Space and Technology, 102d Cong. 2d Sess. Report on the Computer Security Act of 1987 (Comm. Print July 1992).

9. *The Computer Security Act of 1987: Hearings before the H.R. Subcomm. on Science, Research and Technology and the Subcomm. on Transportation, Aviation and Materials of the Comm. on Science, Space and Technology*, 100th Cong., 1st Sess. 8 (1987).

10. "Thoughts on the Categorization of Sensitive Unclassified Information, March 19, 1991," Office of Associate Director for Computer Security, U.S. Dept. of Commerce.

11. 5 U.S.C.§ 552 (1991).

12. See, for example, President Ronald Reagan's "Executive Order 12,356, National Security Information," April 2, 1982, 47 *Federal Register* 14874.

13. 5 C.F.R. § 1312.4 (1991).

14. *Freedom of Information Case List* (U.S. Dept. of Justice, Sept. 1990).

15. *Freedom of Information Case List*, 612.

16. *Freedom of Information Case List*, 613.

17. Richard L. Fricker, "Information Please: Is the FOIA a Myth?" *American Bar Association Journal*, June 1990, 57.

18. Divina Paredes-Japa, "Bush Flexes Secrecy Muscles," *The Quill*, October 1991, 28.

19. Christopher Dunn, "Judging Secrets," *Villanova Law Review* 31:471 (1986).

20. Dunn, 510.

21. *EPA v. Mink*, 410 U.S. 73, 93 S.Ct. 827, 35 L.Ed.2d 119, 1 Media L.Rep. 2448 (1973).

22. *Abbotts v. Nuclear Regulatory Commission*, 247 U.S. App. D.C. 114, 766 F.2d 604 (D.C. Cir. 1985).

23. *Abbotts v. Nuclear Regulatory Commission*, 606.

24. Gregory G. Brooker, "FOIA Exemption 3 and the CIA," *Minnesota Law Review* 68:1231 (1984).

25. Michael H. Hughes, "CIA v. Sims: Supreme Court Deference to Agency Interpretation of FOIA Exemption 3," *Catholic University Law Review* 35:279 (1985).

26. *CIA v. Sims*, 471 U.S. 159, 105 S.Ct. 1881, 85 L.Ed.2d 173, 11 Media L.Rep. 2017 (1985).

27. Maria H. Benecki, "Developments Under the Freedom of Information Act," *Duke Law Journal* 1988:566 (1988).

28. 26 U.S.C. §6103 (1982).

29. 18 U.S.C. §1905 (1982).

30. Each of the U.S. Presidents since the 1940s has issued such a directive. Reagan's order superseded President Carter's 1978 Executive Order 12,065, which specified, "If there is reasonable doubt which designation is appropriate, or whether the information should be classified at all, the less restrictive designation should be used, or the information should not be classified."

31. Donna Demac, *Keeping America Uninformed* (N.Y.: Pilgrim Press, 1984).

32. Exec. Order No.12,356 §1.1(c).

33. Exec. Order No.12,356, §1.4(a).

34. Demac, 14.

35. Exec. Order No. 12,356 §1.6(d).

36. Demac, 17.

37. *Freedom of Information Case List*, 398.

38. Presidential directives, unlike executive orders, are not required to be published in the *Federal Register* and so might not be publicly known unless entered into a public record for some other reason. In this case, congressional hearings on the meaning of language contained in the proposed Computer Security Act brought N.S.D.D. to light.

39. Jack W. Simpson, *Online*, 11 (4):7 (July 1987).

40. Simpson, 8.

41. National Telecommunications and Information Systems Security Committee (NTISSC) Directive No. 2. John M. Poindexter was chairman of the NTISSC and personal adviser to President Reagan.

42. *The Computer Security Act of 1987: Hearings before the Subcommittee on Science, Research and Technology*, 100th Cong. 1st Sess. 8 (1987), 38.

43. *Computer Security Act: Hearings*, 39.

44. *Computer Security Research and Training Act of 1985: Hearing Before a Subcomm. of the H.R. Comm. on Government Operations*, 99th Cong., 1st Sess. (Sept. 18, 1985). (*Computer Research Hearing*)

45. H.R. 2889 (1985).

46. *Computer Research Hearings*, 1.

47. *Computer Research Hearings*, 2, 8-10.

48. *Computer Research Hearings*, 9.

49. *Computer Research Hearings*, 9-13.

50. H.R. Rep.No. 753, 99th Cong., 2d Sess. (1986).

51. Rep.No. 753, 8.

52. Rep. No. 753, pt.2, 9.

53. *Computer Security Act of 1987: Hearings Before a Subcomm. of the H.R. Comm. on Government Operations*, 100th Cong., 1st Sess. (1987) (*Government Operations Hearing*); *Computer Security Act of 1987: Hearings Before the Subcomm. on Science, Research and Technology and the Subcomm. on Transportation, Aviation and Materials of the H.R. Comm. on Science, Space and Technology*, 100th Cong., 1st Sess.8 (1987). (*Science, Space Hearing*)

54. H.R. Rep. No. 153, 100th Cong. 1st Sess., pt.1 (1987).

55. *Government Operations Hearings*, 486, correspondence dated April 9, 1987.

56. *Government Operations Hearings*, 7.

57. *Government Operations Hearings*, 106.

58. *Computer Security Act of 1987*, 101 Stat. 1727.

59. 101 Stat. 1730.

60. 101 Stat. 1724.

61. *1989 Annual Report of the National Computer System Security and Privacy Advisory Board* (March 1990) 1.

62. *Implementation of the Computer Security Act: Hearing Before the Subcomm. on Transportation, Aviation and Materials of the H.R. Comm. on Science, Space and Technology*, 100th Cong., 2d Sess. 146 (1988).

63. *Implementation Hearing*, 102 (1988).

64. *Implementation Hearing*, 103 (1988). The Navy reported 27,000 "sensitive" systems (one half of the systems reported); the Army had 12,000 systems; the Air Force 10,000; all civilian agencies reported about 1,400 systems, or about 3 percent of the total.

65. *Implementation of the Computer Security Act: Hearings Before the Subcomm. on Transportation, Aviation and Materials and the Subcomm. on Science, Research and Technology of the H.R. Comm. on Science, Space and Technology*, 101st Cong., 1st Sess. 18 (1989).

66. *Implementation Hearings*, 25 (1989).

67. *Military and Civilian Control of Computer Security Issues: Hearing Before the Legislation and National Security Subcomm. of the H.R. Comm. on Government Operations*, 101st Cong., 1st Sess. 2-3 (1989).

68. *Military and Civilian Control Hearing*, 3.

69. *Military and Civilian Control Hearing*, 3.

70. *Military and Civilian Control Hearing*, 61.

71. *Military and Civilian Control Hearing*, 61.

72. *Military and Civilian Control Hearing*, 287.

73. *Implementation of the Computer Security Act: Hearing Before the Subcomm. on Transportation, Aviation and Materials of the H.R. Comm. on Science, Space and Technology*, 101st Cong., 2d Sess., 137 (1990).

74. Clifford Stoll, *The Cuckoo's Egg* (N.Y.: Doubleday, 1989).

75. *Implementation Hearing*, 22 (1990).

76. *Implementation Hearing*, 18 (1990).

77. *Implementation Hearing*, 25 (1990).

78. *Implementation Hearing*, 27 (1990).

79. "Thoughts on the Categorization of Sensitive Unclassified Information," March 19, 1991, Office of Associate Director for Computer Security, U.S. Dept. of Commerce.

80. "Thoughts on the Categorization," 1-2.

81. *Computer Security: Hearing Before the Subcomm. on Technology and Competitiveness of the H.R. Comm. on Science, Space and Technology*, 102d Cong., 1st Sess., No. 42, 9 (1991).

82. *Computer Security Hearing*, 10 (1991).

83. *Computer Security Hearing*, 11 (1991).

84. *Computer Security Hearing*, 12 (1991).

85. *Computer Security Hearing*, 12 (1991).

86. Telephone interview September 16, 1991 and April 19, 1994.

87. Dunn, "Judging Secrets," 472.

88. Telephone interview November 8, 1990.

Chapter 5

The Pentagon Rules on Media Access

INTRODUCTION

Since the Persian Gulf War in 1991, several U.S. journalists have published books decrying the restrictions placed on the media during the war[1] and several reports have been compiled that review the U.S. policies restricting media access during military action.[2] Conflicting views about how the media should report military activity are not new.[3] But the Persian Gulf War, following so closely on the heels of the Panama and Grenada military actions,[4] sparked renewed attention that seemed to be driven by the media's recent technological advances—nearly instantaneous reporting and broadcasting from anywhere to anywhere.[5]

Congress had debated the merits of executive branch information control and the use of media pools after U.S. military involvement in Panama and Grenada.[6] Immediately before the Persian Gulf War, Congress again addressed the question of how much and what kind of executive branch information control should be permitted.[7] Formal guidelines for media access "in the event of hostilities in the Persian Gulf" were issued January 4, 1991, by the Department of Defense.[8] Ultimately, on January 14, Congress gave the executive branch and the Department of Defense approval in managing all information control matters relevant to a successful Desert Storm action.[9] But after the allies declared they had won the Persian Gulf War, there were some regrets expressed by members of Congress about the way war information had been handled.[10]

This chapter reviews the congressional considerations of executive branch information control in the months before and after the Persian Gulf War; reviews congressional debates about the policy of limiting or controlling media access to military information; and chronicles the characterizations by congressional members of news information. These characterizations are categorized in this chapter as either content-centered or conduit-centered, and as either inhibiting or enhancing the U.S. government's operation. The summary draws together those characterizations found in the hearings.

It is useful first, however, to review briefly the modern history of U.S. media controls during other off-shore conflicts of the 1980s in order to understand to what congressional leaders are referring in the subsequent hearings and testimony. Obviously, there have been no on-shore military conflicts recently in the United States requiring media pools which this study could examine. Off-shore conflicts are selected, instead, for this study for a number of reasons. Off-shore conflicts are generally thought to be less imminently threatening to the United States than an on-shore or internal military conflict, and therefore would probably be rationalized or defended rhetorically very differently than an on-shore, immediately threatening military conflict. An off-shore conflict, too, because it is probably less threatening would call for less stringent rules about information flow.[11]

BRIEF HISTORY OF MODERN U.S. MEDIA CONTROLS DURING OFF-SHORE CONFLICTS

After the Vietnam experience during the 1960s, some political and military leaders looked for a new model of information control for use with news media representatives, one that would keep U.S. public support high during an off-shore conflict.[12] And the Thatcher government provided just such a model during the 1982 Falkland Islands conflict between Great Britain and Argentina.[13] The British model included controlling media access to military theaters and excluding journalists who might not submit positive stories about domestic efforts, as well as sanitizing visual images of war. Great Britain has historically maintained, and does so even today, some of the same press restrictions that prompted the authors of the United States Constitution to add the First Amendment's free press clause 200 years ago. And yet the press restrictions used for the Falkland Islands conflict can be found in U.S. policy during every off-shore conflict since 1982.[14]

On October 25, 1983, President Ronald Reagan ordered U.S. troops to invade Grenada, an island in the Caribbean. No American news media representatives accompanied the invasion, in part because the operation was planned in secrecy and executed as a surprise. The specific exclusion of the media was the order of the chairman of the Joint Chiefs of Staff, General John W. Vessey, Jr.[15] The day after the invasion, media complaints prompted some efforts to accommodate journalists in Barbados by establishing there a Joint Information Bureau. Media pools for visiting Grenada on October 27 were organized and supervised by the U.S. military.[16] But media representatives complained about the limited, controlled access that military personnel allowed reporters. As a consequence of a Department of Defense panel report[17] following the Grenada invasion, the assistant secretary of defense was directed to form a stand-by press pool for activation during initial stages of any surprise military operations.[18]

The most significant call on the press pool occurred shortly after the U.S. military invasion of Panama on December 20, 1989. Again the media complained about restricted access to the action in Panama. The pool members were detained so that by the time they reached the scene nearly all the military objectives were completed and there were practically no first-hand news reports of the action.[19]

Some complaints were registered in Congress about the military's handling of the media during the Grenada and Panama invasions, but the most striking complaint is contained in the March 17, 1988, Senate record that reported news—solely through newspaper clippings—of the U.S. deployment of troops to Honduras.[20] House Majority Whip Tony Colero of California is quoted as complaining, "Nothing that we have heard today justifies the sending of young men into the jungles of Central America. . . . We have been notified [of U.S. military action] by the press every inch of the way. The White House hasn't had the decency to call the leadership of the House or the Senate."[21] This concern could be characterized as focusing on the content of the information rather than the way in which the information was carried—content-centered, rather than conduit-centered. The complaint seems to be that Congress was no better informed than the press at this point, and that the White House had more details than it was sharing with the House or the Senate.

The Department of Defense reviewed the complaints about the treatment of the media and media access during off-shore conflict, and responded in 1990 with an in-house report that included 17 corrective recommendations.[22] These included suggestions that the military's public affairs officer "weigh in heavily with the Secretary of Defense . . . to overcome any secrecy or other obstacles blocking prompt deployment of a pool to the scene of action";[23] that "safety of the pool members must not be used as a reason to keep the pool from action";[24] and that "the national media pool should never again be herded as a single unwieldy unit."[25] The assistant secretary for public affairs indicated that some of the points needed refinement, and that some were under consideration.[26] As hostilities in the Persian Gulf increased later that year, there were some negotiations with the news community[27] before the Defense Department issued ground rules and guidelines for correspondents in the event of a new conflict.[28]

CONGRESSIONAL REVIEW OF MEDIA ACCESS IMMEDIATELY BEFORE THE PERSIAN GULF WAR

Three months before the outbreak of Persian Gulf hostilities, Congress heard testimony on May 9, 1990, about poor access to information about military actions during the Panama invasion.[29] "Civilian suffering and death is still not reported. Network TV coverage of the invasion was United States military video fed to the 'press pool' holed up in the United States embassy,"[30] reported Representative Ted Weiss, citing news articles in January and February issues of *The New York Times* and *The Nation*. But there was no move to impose corrective measures on the military's rule over media access. This complaint might be characterized as one that is about information content rather than the means of transferring the information; the focus of interest was on data availability rather than narrowly on media access to available information.

Immediately after the invasion of Kuwait by Iraq on August 2, Congress held a joint hearing[31] to examine the impact of the Persian Gulf crisis on U.S. interests. Among the considerations were the kind and amount of information the executive branch was required to transmit to Congress about the specifics of U.S. economic, diplomatic and military actions against Iraq.[32] For instance, Rep. Lee Hamilton, a Democrat from Indiana, asked Department of Defense assistant secretary Henry S. Rowen about the existence and substance of any military agreements with Saudi Arabia. What he learned was that an agreement did exist between the U.S. executive branch and the Saudi government, about which Congress knew nothing.[33]

When Representative Hamilton asked when the substance of the agreement would be made known to Congress, Rowen replied, "I do not know the timing of that, sir. We will certainly let you know on that." Representative Hamilton continued, "Well, will we [Congress] get it in the next week or ten years from now?" John Kelly, assistant secretary in the State Department, answered for Rowen, "Certainly not ten years from now. The Case-Zablocki Act, it is my recollection, requires sub-mission within 60 days."[34]

Throughout the hearings there were references to media reports that contradicted the military representatives' testimony.[35] Congres-sional rancor was evident over the substance or content of the reports, not over the means of transmitting the reports, as military personnel tried to hedge, under report military activities, and then cite the repres-sion of press freedoms by governments in the Gulf region as a rationale for U.S. military activities there.[36] When Representative Hamilton asked Assistant Secretary Kelly whether Kelly expected changes in the political systems of the Middle East after U.S.-sponsored support in the area, it was somewhat ironic that Kelly said, "I think that's right and we are seeing it already in terms of press availabilities, press freedoms and so on."[37]

Congress continued to find military experts alternately dodging and embroidering their reports. During the testimony of retired General William E. Odom in a November hearing, Senator Strom Thurmond, of South Carolina, noted the disparity between retired military officers' pessimistic views and active duty officers' optimistic views. "I see it in their editorials in the press. . . . [but] Can you explain why, when testifying in uniform, our officers are always optimistic about our capabilities; yet when retired, some of them take the opposite view?"[38] General Odom candidly replied, "I think it has to do with the fact that you control the money, sir."[39]

Even in December, Congress still found itself reliant on media reports, rather than U.S. military reports made to Congress, for some specific information on activities in the Gulf region.[40] For example, the committee report contained references such as, "In late October, press reports suggested that additional force requirements were being con-sidered by the Chairman of the Joint Chiefs of Staff . . . ," and, "On December 26, *The Wall Street Journal* reported that according to Pentagon officials . . ."[41]

Some members of Congress decided in early January to speak out against the executive branch information controls, and proposed a resolution calling for the submission of certain information regarding Operation Desert Shield.[42] The measure was referred to committees on foreign affairs and armed services, as was a similar bill in February.[43] Congress was clearly able to act on its desire for information about the war from the executive branch, but allowed the Pentagon Rules on Media Access, issued weeks before the air strikes, to stand.[44]

For example, the "Resolution relating to press coverage of military actions in the Persian Gulf" submitted by Representative Barbara Boxer on January 18 failed to win much attention. Her plea to members of Congress as late as January 22 titled, "We Cannot Promote Democracy with Censorship," urged action against "unwarranted prior restraint on the abilities of the United States news media to report . . . unfolding events to the American public."[45] The resolution cited the Department of Defense intention to "institute a policy of selective coverage by limiting the access of the news media . . ." and indicated that "the Department of Defense has apparently prevented accredited correspondents from covering the initiation of combat to prevent the disclosure of politically embarrassing information."[46] But the resolution received no action after referral to the House Committee on Armed Services.

On February 20, 1991, after the air war had begun and just days before the ground war, a Senate committee hearing began on the subject of the Pentagon Rules.[47] Senator John Glenn, of Ohio, noted in an opening statement, "There are many complaints about the 'pool' system and the extent to which 'escorts' have become 'minders' cutting off interviews mid-sentence, in addition to conducting after-the-fact security review."[48] Senator Glenn added, "An independent press insures [sic] that the public has the information it needs [during war] to exercise its rights as citizens." But he asked, "How do we insure [sic] a balance . . . between the public's right to know and the military's need for security?"[49]

Congress, it seems, was well aware of the problems of media access to the conflict and by inaction, it could be construed, supported the military establishment's solution by offering an argument that cited safety for troops, reporters and the nation at large.[50] For example, Senator William Roth of Delaware cited the media satellite technology as creating a "'war of the airwaves' . . . in each of our living rooms." He went on to say, "We are quickly learning that in a war like this of words and satellites, between democracies and a dictatorship, the dictatorship will have the propaganda advantage every time."[51] Senator Roth concluded his remarks, however, by saying,

> Like many Americans, I share the concern that the safety of
> our men and women in the Gulf not be compromised in any
> way by press reports. . . . I believe our military leadership is
> trying to do its best to provide the news media with access to
> information without betraying any information which might be
> useful to the enemy.[52]

The components of the discussion among the committee members
providing testimony weighed a free press and the right of the people to
know what government was doing, against military success and the
protection of the soldiers in combat.[53] The reasons for limiting access
supplied to Congress during this and subsequent hearings by military
strategists had more to do with the timeliness of transmitting a report,
while the reasons for censorship after a report had been prepared had
to do with the content of the information. In these reasons can be
found the difference between access and censorship—the first line of
control is in access to information, but if that fails, then censorship of
transmission can be useful, both military and political strategists suggested.[54]

In testimony given before the joint congressional committee, the
military establishment clearly saw the advantages of limiting access
rather than censoring. In August 1990, the U.S. Central Command
headquarters began putting together the revised ground rules that
would become the new model for Desert Shield press pools.[55] Among
the concerns expressed was that "the enemy . . . can be expected . . . [to
plant] inaccurate data with selected media representatives or organizations . . . to adversely influence public opinion."[56] This, of course, is a
concern with information content, but the ground rules go on to stress
that information release will be governed at all times by the guiding
rule that "security at the source will be the policy."[57] In addition, the
guidelines say that the basic principle governing the release of information was to be "that all information that is consistent with operational
security and does not compromise the safety of United States or
friendly nation personnel will be made available to [news media] and
the American public."

Pete Williams, Assistant Secretary of Defense for Public Affairs,
characterized the problem of press pools as one of simply "rubbing
reporters the wrong way."[58] Reporters, he said, are accustomed to
working on their own. "The best are especially independent."[59] He
went on to say that the pool system does allow a reasonable number of
journalists to see the action, and "that the American people will get the

accounting they deserve." Williams closed his remarks to the committee by citing General Dwight D. Eisenhower's "Regulations for War Correspondents" as providing succinct support for the present system.

> The first essential in military operations is that no information of value should be given to the enemy. The first essential in newspaper work and broadcasting is wide-open publicity. It is your job and mine to try to reconcile these sometimes diverse considerations.[60]

What Williams failed to mention, however, was that during Eisenhower's time reporters were permitted to report individually what they saw as they saw fit, rather than only as part of modern press pools.

Williams did respond to questions comparing World War II media activity with Persian Gulf media restrictions by suggesting that the restrictions were in place to protect the media personnel from the dangers of front-line conflict and because the logistics of travel to and from the front were so much more difficult and dangerous in the Gulf than during previous wars.[61] This kind of concern might be characterized as one that is conduit-centered—concern with the information carrier. This concern has the effect, ultimately, of controlling information content by controlling information access.

During the hearings retired U.S. Army Major General Winant Sidle suggested that the government should think of the media as neither lap dog nor attack dog, but rather as watchdog. "Mutual antagonism and distrust are not in the best interests of the media, the military or the American people," he told the committee.[62] The ostensible concern Sidle expressed was for the carrier of information, though the ultimate imposition could be on information content.

Sidle went on to remind the military, however, that the "military is funded by taxpayer dollars and the taxpayers have a right to know what the military is doing with a few exceptions. . . . The only way for the military to both inform the taxpayers and to get credit for doing a good job is through the news media."[63] His concern here was, as before, with the results of information content, but seemed to assume only one means of carrier.

Another retired U.S. Army officer, Col. Harry G. Summers, Jr., served as a senior military correspondent for *U.S. News and World Report* during the Persian Gulf War. He told the committee that he thought the American people were better informed, meaning, he said, more immediately informed, about the Persian Gulf crisis than they had been about past conflicts.[64]

Colonel Summers also said, "I think that pool restrictions on the press are dumb. They create the erroneous impression that the military has something to hide."[65] He suggested that reporters should have "total freedom to see all that we are doing, realizing the transmission might have to be delayed for security reasons." Summers suggested that information content should only be delayed, but that the information conduits or carriers—reporters—be given wide access. Though his view could have carried considerable weight, given his experience as both a ranking military officer and a media representative, the committee made no recommendation to eliminate press pools during either the Persian Gulf War or subsequent conflicts.

The following are examples of the kinds of information that came to light after the Persian Gulf War:[66]

*About one-third of American troop deaths resulted from "friendly" fire ("U.S. works to cut 'friendly fire' deaths," *News and Observer*, Raleigh, N.C., December 9, 1991, A3);

*Only about one weapon in ten was a precision-guided weapon; the rest were regular mass destruction weapons ("Pentagon acknowledges," *Herald-Sun*, Durham, N.C., February 13, 1991, A7);

*Several thousand Iraq civilians died ("Bombing puts U.S.," *News and Observer*, Raleigh, N.C., February 14, 1991, A1);

*That much vaunted equipment, such as the expensive invisible B2 bomber is, in fact, visible and a poor performer, that U.S. tanks, distracted by sand, had trouble distinguishing friend from enemy, and that some technical systems did not perform to par ("Army's top war machines," Associated Press, January 9, 1992).

CONCLUSIONS

The concerns expressed by Congress, military and executive branch staff members focused on the conduit or carrier of the information—the reporter in the field. The restrictions of pools were justified in terms of safety and convenience for media and military personnel. Members of the media have challenged the Pentagon Rules since the end of the Persian Gulf War,[67] but Congress has not acted in any substantive way to countermand the guidelines.

In the chapters so far, evidence was sought that suggested a cohesive understanding of the concept of information and the ways in which information can be effectively controlled. The concept, congressional debate suggests, can be divided into concerns about information as content and information carriers or conduits. Control of information content can effectively occur at the point of origination—the first carrier or conduit—as noted in both Foreign Agents Registration Act debates and the memos accompanying the Pentagon Rules for Media Access. The information content controlled by the Computer Security Act is that information contained in computer databases, another kind of carrier for information storage and retrieval.

In Chapter 6, a discussion of traditional ethical principles sets up the frame on which to evaluate the kind of legal information controls described in the previous chapters. Chapter 7 works through some of the debate already described here in terms of such principles, and Chapter 8 suggests a policy for information control in the technological age in which the modern United States now finds itself.

NOTES

1. See, for example, John R. MacArthur, *Second Front: Censorship and Propaganda in the Gulf War* (New York: Hill and Wang, 1992) and John J. Fialka, *Hotel Warriors* (Baltimore: Johns Hopkins University Press/ Washington, D.C.: The Woodrow Wilson Center Press, 1992).

2. For example, *The Media At War: The Press and the Persian Gulf Conflict* (New York: Gannett Foundation Media Center, 1991) and *Pentagon Rules on Media Access to the Persian Gulf War: Hearings Before the Senate Comm. on Governmental Affairs*, 102d Cong., 1st Sess. (1991). (*Pentagon Rules*)

3. See William M. Hammond, "The Army and Public Affairs: A Glance Back," in *Newsmen & National Defense: Is Conflict Inevitable?* ed. Lloyd J. Matthews (New York: Macmillan, 1991) 1-18; Phillip Knightley, *The First Casualty* (New York: Harcourt Brace Jovanovich, 1975); James Russell Wiggins, *Freedom or Secrecy* (New York: Oxford University Press, 1964); Kent Cooper, *The Right to Know* (New York: Farrar, Strauss & Cudahy, 1956).

4. See Jacqueline Sharkey, *Under Fire: U.S. Military Restrictions on the Media from Grenada to the Persian Gulf* (Washington, D.C.: The Center for Public Integrity, 1991).

5. See Steven Komarow, "Pooling Around in Panama," *Washington Journalism Review*, March 1990, 45; Fred S. Hoffman, "Review of Panama Pool Deployment, December, 1989," (Hoffman Report), Office of the Assistant Secretary for Public Affairs, U.S. Department of Defense, March 1990; Background paper by Peter Braestrup, Sidle Report August 23, 1984, in *Battle Lines, Report of the Twentieth Century Fund Task Force on the Military and*

the Media (New York: Priority Press, 1985).

6. *Hearings Before the Subcomm. on Courts, Civil Liberties and the Administration of Justice of the House Comm. on the Judiciary*, 98th Cong., 2d Sess. 3 (1983); 134 *Cong.Rec.* S2440 (1988); 136 *Cong.Rec.* E1442 (May 9, 1990).

7. See H.R.Rep.No. 102-5 Part 2, 102d Cong., 1st Sess. (1990).

8. *Pentagon Rules on Media Access to the Persian Gulf War: Hearings Before the Senate Committee on Governmental Affairs*, 102 Cong., 1st Sess. 301 (1991). *(Pentagon Rules)*

9. *Authorization for the Use of Force Pursuant to United Nations Security Council Resolution 678*, P.L.No. 102-1, 105 Stat. 3 (1991).

10. *Pentagon Rules*.

11. For a history of press controls before the mid-20th century, see James Russell Wiggins, *Freedom or Secrecy*, revised ed. (New York: Oxford University Press, 1964); Jack A. Gottschalk, "Consistent with Security," *Communications and the Law* 5:36 (Summer 1983); Phillip Knightley, *The First Casualty* (New York: Harcourt, Brace, Jovanovich, 1975); Robert E. Summers (ed.), *Wartime Censorship of Press and Radio* (New York: The H.W. Wilson Company, 1942); *Battle Lines, Twentieth Century Fund Task Force on the Military and the Media* (New York: Priority Press, 1985).

12. Sharkey, *Under Fire*, 4.

13. Naval Lt. Cmdr. Arthur A. Humphries, "Two Routes to the Wrong Destination: Public Affairs in the South Atlantic War," *Naval War College Review*, June 1983. Also discussed in *Battle Lines*, ch.5.

14. Sharkey, 23.

15. *Battle Lines*, 90.

16. *Battle Lines*, 94.

17. U.S. Department of Defense, *Report by the CJCS Media-Military Relations Panel (Sidle Panel)* (Washington, D.C., undated) reproduced in *Battle Lines*.

18. Fred Hiatt, "Pentagon Plans Media Pool to Cover Missions," *Washington Post*, August 24, 1984, A1.

19. Michael Specter, "Panama: Firsthand Coverage and Secondhand Diplomacy—News Organizations Struggle with 'Pool' Format," *Washington Post*, December 21, 1989, D1, and December 22, 1989, A29.

20. 134 *Cong. Rec.* S.4224, 100th Cong., 2d Sess. (1988).

21. 134 *Cong. Rec.* S.4283.

22. Fred S. Hoffman, *Review of Panama Pool Deployment, December 1989* (Washington, D.C.: Department of Defense, March 1990).

23. Hoffman, *Review of Panama Pool Deployment*, 17.

24. Hoffman, *Review of Panama Pool Deployment*.

25. Hoffman, *Review of Panama Pool Deployment*, 18.

26. Patrick E. Tyler, "Officially, Pentagon Takes Blame," *Washington Post*, March 21, 1990, A19.

27. Howard Kurtz, "Pentagon to Ease Coverage Rules," *Washington Post*,

January 5, 1991, A20.

28. Howard Kurtz, "Pentagon Sets Rules for War Reporting," *Washington Post*, January 10, 1991, A25.

29. 136 *Cong. Rec.* E1442, 101st Cong. 2d Sess. (1990).

30. 136 *Cong. Rec.*, E1443 (1990).

31. *The Persian Gulf Crisis: Joint Hearings Before the Subcomms. on Arms Control, International Security and Science, Europe and the Middle East, and on International Operations of the House Comm. on Foreign Affairs and the Joint Economic Comm.*, 101st Cong., 2d Sess. (1990).

32. *Persian Gulf Crisis*, 101st Cong., 2d Sess. (1990).

33. *Persian Gulf Crisis*, 94.

34. *Persian Gulf Crisis*.

35. *Persian Gulf Crisis*, 97, 99, 103, 131, 135.

36. *Persian Gulf Crisis*, 129.

37. *Persian Gulf Crisis*.

38. *Crisis in the Persian Gulf Region: U.S. Policy Options and Implications: Hearings Before the Senate Comm. on Armed Services*, 101st Cong., 2d Sess. (1990).

39. *Crisis in the Persian Gulf*, 501.

40. *Crisis in the Persian Gulf: Sanctions, Diplomacy and War: Hearings Before the H.R. Comm. on Armed Services*, 101st Cong., 2d Sess. 893 (1990).

41. *Crisis in the Persian Gulf: Sanctions*, 893.

42. H.Res.19, 102d Cong., 1st Sess. (1991).

43. *An Act to Require Regular Reports to the Congress on the Costs to the United States of Operation Desert Shield and Operation Desert Storm*, H.R. 586, 102d Cong., 1st Sess. (1991).

44. H.R. Res. 37, 102d Cong., 1st Sess.(1991).

45. 137 *Cong. Rec.*, H.73 (1991).

46. 137 *Cong. Rec.*, 74.

47. *Pentagon Rules on Media Access to the Persian Gulf War: Hearings Before the Senate Comm. on Governmental Affairs*, 102d Cong., 1st Sess. (1991).

48. *Pentagon Rules*, 2.

49. *Pentagon Rules*, 2.

50. *Pentagon Rules*, 4-5.

51. *Pentagon Rules*, 4.

52. *Pentagon Rules*, 4.

53. *Pentagon Rules*, 6.

54. U.S. Army Major General Winant Sidle testimony, in *Pentagon Rules*, 53; also, Sharkey, *Under Fire*, 23-37.

55. *Pentagon Rules*, 279.

56. *Pentagon Rules*, 280.

57. *Pentagon Rules*, 285.

58. *Pentagon Rules*, 13.

59. *Pentagon Rules*.

60. *Pentagon Rules*, 13.

61. *Pentagon Rules*, 15.

62. *Pentagon Rules*, 54.

63. *Pentagon Rules*.

64. *Pentagon Rules*, 56.

65. *Pentagon Rules*.

66. For a more complete list and discussion, see, Donald L. Shaw and Shannon Martin, "The Natural and Inevitable Three Phases of War Reporting," *The Media and the Persian Gulf War*, Robert E. Denton, ed. (Westport, Conn.: Praeger, 1993).

67. Jason DeParle, "Long Series of Military Decisions Led to Gulf War News Censorship," *New York Times*, May 5, 1991, A1 and "Keeping the News in Step: Are the Pentagon's Gulf War Rules Here to Stay?" *New York Times*, May 6, 1991, A9.

Chapter 6

Principles of Ethical Reasoning

INTRODUCTION

When government must choose, within the frame of the U.S. Constitution, among the pros and cons of information access and of information control then often the decisions are not easy.[1] The conflicting benefits and harms of access and control are difficult to weigh, in part, because there are no clear constitutional guidelines for tallying each of their separate values. And so government must discover and determine a winner in each new clash that occurs between access and control. Often, too, the rationale for these determinations is forged from past practice in the law and from ethical principles evolving out of various perspectives.

This chapter provides a systematic way, using traditional ethical theories, of thinking about the dichotomy of information access and information control that has been described in earlier chapters. A fundamental premise for the following discussion, however, is that sometimes there is a difference between that which one or another branch of the government has a right to do (law) and that which is the right thing to do (ethics).[2] The brief review of traditional ethical theories in this chapter will provide a framework in which to place the kinds of concerns that were observed about information access and information control in the three examples examined in Chapters 3, 4 and 5.

INFORMATION FLOW REVISITED

The Foreign Agents Registration Act, as was mentioned in Chapter 3, originally was designed to track and control information carriers—those from or representing foreign government interests. But this statutory law was also found by some members of Congress to control—or selectively bar—information content that the United States government simply did not want available to U.S. citizens. The information flow in this case might be characterized as moving from outside the U.S. domain to within the U.S.

The Computer Security Act sprang from an executive branch concern for control over information access but the means of control was through the information carrier—the computer and its users. The law eventually was enacted by Congress, but the original language and concerns expressed by the executive branch remain in its text. The information flow in this case was from inside the U.S. government's domain to citizens also within the U.S. government domain.

The Pentagon Media Rules during the recent Grenada, Panama and Persian Gulf conflicts were designed to control information content by controlling the kind of access reporters had to information sources—a kind of carrier control. The information flow here was from inside U.S. military controlled areas that were outside the United States to those U.S. citizens within the United States.

These three examples encompass the ways information can travel or flow to U.S. citizens, with interruption by the federal government. These are only cited as examples and not as either unique or all-encompassing. The point here is to provide a variety of avenues for the discussion of the kinds of government action taken in the recent past, and for the design of an effective information access and control policy.

ETHICS IN GOVERNMENT

While some attempts have been made most recently to adopt ethics standards among government officials[3] that fill the gap between clearly illegal behavior and universally acceptable behavior,[4] often the standards or policies of individual groups, such as journalists, rely on experience, tradition, and a polyglot of maxims.[5] There is evidence in the arguments offered by legislators to use moral justifications for one action or another in decisions about information control and access. In Chapter 7 these ethical, or moral, justifications are specifically culled from testimony in order to understand whether modern justifications are ethically different from the kind used by the founding framers writing constitutional guidelines and by some more modern scholars of First Amendment theories.

The use of systematic ethical theories of the sort associated with classic education, however, could be thought of as fundamental in establishing ethics standards for professional groups and government, rather than as a last resort.[6] Such theories, generally, are devised to separate right action from wrong action, rather than legal from illegal action, and so they should be a natural first place to turn for behavioral advice.

GENERAL THEORIES OF ETHICAL REASONING

Ethical theories in Western philosophical thought are at least twenty-five centuries old. The space constraints here will not allow surveying them all or applying all of them to particular cases. Two important kinds of theories are briefly described: teleological theories and deontological theories. The teleological theories look solely to an act's results or outcomes in evaluating the rightness or wrongnes of an act. Deontological theories look at other factors, such as obligations and duties, in evaluating the rightness or wrongness of an act. These two kinds of theories are in many ways opposed to one another and will allow some diversity of theory within a brief space.

DEONTOLOGICAL ETHICS

"Deontology" is derived from the Greek words *deon* meaning duty and *logos* meaning science. Consequently, deontology is sometimes referred to as the science of duty. More specifically, deontological theories of ethics suggest that at least some acts are morally obligatory regardless of their consequences for specific human beings.

Immanuel Kant (1724-1804) is usually thought of as espousing a deontological, or duty-driven theory.[7] Such a theory holds that an act's consequences do not alone determine whether the act is right or wrong. Other considerations, such as motives and intentions and duties, are thought to be relevant to evaluating an act's moral rightness.

Kant considered consequences, but placed additional weight on the underlying rationale of an action. One of the important hallmarks of a right act, Kant thought, is the universalizability of its underlying principle. By 'universalizability' Kant had in mind weighing a principle in terms of its adoption by all people as a guide to action. General agreement of a principle's universalizability, Kant held, means that the principle or motive for the action could be justified satisfactorily to everyone involved, or was consistent with respect for individuality.

Universalizability seeks to measure the rightness of an act by whether all agents of that act would possibly consent if fully informed of each other's motives. This is sometimes referred to as the categorical imperative. The kind of agreement Kant had in mind was not necessarily real, voiced agreement, but rational agreement by mature, well-informed, ideal agents. This provided for varying degrees of intellectual growth or self-consciousness.

TELEOLOGICAL ETHICS

"Teleology" is derived from the Greek word *teleo*, meaning end. Teleology is the study of ends or final causes. A common feature of teleological theories of ethics is that less emphasis is placed on duty and moral obligations and more on good or desirable consequences for human beings. One modern teleological theory of ethics is that of utilitarianism.

John Stuart Mill (1806-1873) is often thought of as providing a mature statement of utilitarianism, an ethical theory also propounded by Jeremy Bentham (1748-1832) and James Mill (1773-1836). Utilitarianism is a teleological or ends-driven theory. Roughly, utilitarianism claims that the degree of rightness of an act depends on its utility, that is, on the amount of benefit of its consequences, rather than on motives or duties.

A full statement of a particular utilitarian view would need to characterize benefit, which is often identified with happiness, and give some way of measuring it quantitatively. That is, the utilitarian needs to say what a beneficial consequence is, and how to adjudicate among competing goods, and then how to measure goods across a population of recipients. Since we most often act without full knowledge of consequences, utilitarians also need to say something about expected benefit, especially when it differs from actual or realized benefit.

John Stuart Mill identifies an act's resulting benefit as the greatest happiness for the greatest number of people. For him, therefore, it is general welfare which is paramount, and an act is the right one if it promotes the general welfare. For the utilitarian an act, for example, of killing is right or wrong depending on whether or not its consequences increase happiness for the community generally.

Kant differs from John Stuart Mill, then, in evaluating moral rightness in terms other than the greatest happiness for the greatest number of people. Even if a particular killing—of a despot leader, for example—increases human happiness and the general welfare, this does not guarantee its rightness for Kant. If the sanctity of the individual is an absolute value, then the deontologist can never justify killing, no matter how much general happiness results.

Utilitarians are often divided into subsets. Those who are inclined to judge each act individually within its own particular context are called "act-utilitarians." Those who judge an act in terms of the benefit gained from the general pattern of which it is an instance are "rule-utilitarians." The rule-utilitarian judges an act by first judging whether the rule it follows leads to benefit; if the rule is beneficial, then acts which fall under it are thought to be right. The act-utilitarian, in contrast, judges the act directly by asking whether this particular, unique act leads to benefit; if so, then it is thought to be right. But both kinds of utilitarians determine moral value in terms of the ends achieved.

APPLICATIONS

The initial aim here is not to solve the ethical questions posed by particular situations, but rather to point to how ethical theories can be applied to particular questions about information access and information control. To do this adequately, the principles of First Amendment theory, which have often pointed to social values of information access, must be brought into perspective with the long-standing Western world normative theories of social behavior just reviewed.

First Amendment Theory

Twentieth century First Amendment theories—specifically here, free speech/free press theories—may be thought of in either one of two ways. There are positive, value promoting theories and negative, government restricting theories.[8] These are represented by Alexander Meiklejohn[9] and Thomas Emerson[10] for the positive, and by Ronald Cass[11] and Frederick Schauer[12] for the negative.

Though Meiklejohn contributed an early statement of the positive theory, Emerson is most often quoted for his completeness and general acceptance.[13] Emerson's theory is a system of assumptions underpinning the free speech/free press clause of the First Amendment as it supports the principle of self-governance. His theory, briefly put, says that in order for a society to be self-governed there must be a social mechanism for attaining truth, securing participation from all members in the process of governing, ensuring social control of change and enhancing individual self-fulfillment. Vincent Blasi subsequently emphasized the importance of checking misused official power.[14] The social mechanisms for these ends as cited by Meiklejohn, Emerson and Blasi include a free press.

A positivist describing First Amendment theory might characterize the principle underpinning the theory as that which supports the individual seeking self-fulfillment, or self-actualization, through the attainment of truth. In light of the two ethical theories described earlier in this chapter, the strongest ethics link with the positivist's principles is that of the teleologist John Stuart Mill. Both Mill and the positivist suggest that ultimately society is best served by individuals who are allowed much latitude to express and learn about themselves. The result here, utilitarians might posit, will be the greatest happiness for the greatest number.

Negative free speech/free press theory is a much more recently developed idea and is somewhat less complete than the positive theory. Generally, negative law describes what may not be done, or actions that are prohibited.[15] Briefly, the assumptions underpinning the free speech/free press First Amendment clause as it supports the principle of self-governance are that there must be social mechanisms for scrutinizing the motivations of government[16] and preventing bias, intolerance, self-interest and suppression.[17] Among the social mechanisms for these ends are a free press as an organized means of investigating and publicizing what government is doing or ought to be doing.

A negativist describing First Amendment theory might characterize the principle underpinning the theory as that which prevents government from imposing bias, intolerance, self-interest and suppression. While the primary concern is with discovering motivations within government—a deontological concern—the principle that negativists support is of preventing bad motivations, or keeping bad motivation from affecting the outcomes of governing. Ultimately the concern is with protecting the governed from any motives that act against the individuals' ability to self-govern.

Self-governance could be said to be both the means and the end sought by a society. Since the negativist wants motives for change left out of the process altogether, teleological concerns about outcomes are focal. The result here, for the negativist, is that motives will not play a significant part in determining the appropriate course of specific action by the government because all motives will be scrutinized, criticized and found to be unacceptable by some group, rendering those motives not unanimously adoptable.

FEDERAL INFORMATION CONTROLS

The sorting of ethical principles found in First Amendment theories is one way to begin thinking through possible appropriate ethical principles for laws concerning federal information control. While it might be a logically prior task, there is little or no evidence that such work has been done. However, some observations about possible applications of ethical theories can be made by working through a review of the three government actions described in earlier chapters.

Foreign Agents Registration Act

The Foreign Agents Registration Act declares that its purpose is to protect national defense, internal security and foreign relations by requiring public disclosure of those engaged in propaganda acts.[18] The requirement of public disclosure here might be characterized as the means to an end, that end being promoting the general welfare and safety of the nation. The requirement of public disclosure by the act of filing as a foreign agent, however, might also be characterized as a requirement for individuals to give up some free speech rights, those rights contained in the First Amendment. Giving up this right of free speech, a speech without proven harms, might be thought of as ostensibly in the best interest of the general welfare, though certainly not in the best interest of the individual registered.

What is subtly required by FARA is that there exist a general understanding and acceptance of what exactly is in the best interest of the nation as a whole. There must also be a willingness to enforce forfeiture of some individuals' presumptive right to be left alone—that is, the presumptive right to lobby without required public disclosure of one's associates. The motivation of FARA then might fall in line with utilitarian concerns for the greatest happiness for the greatest number of people in a very broad sense, and the underlying principle would be among those in a teleological model.

But John Stuart Mill, the 19th century scholar of utilitarian principles, framed the ends-driven principles primarily around the individual. Mill asserted that the individual was happiest who was least restricted or controlled by government—this is, the right of man to be left alone—and that it was the collection of these happiest people that made up a collectively happy nation. Mill would have insisted on a careful weighing of individual happinesses. In the case of FARA, important individuals to be considered would be those required to register, and the general happiness would be that of the collective nation. Mill, then, might not have been pleased by many of the requirements[19] of the Foreign Agents Registration Act.

If, however, the underlying principle of U.S. governance is the preservation of the nation above all else, then the motives for implementing means toward the end of national preservation should be examined. Kantians would suggest that one way to evaluate the motives or means would be to discover the general acceptability or universalizability of the those motives or means. That is, would every member of the governed agree with and accept as right the motives or means? This test of universalizability could provide a deontological defense of FARA.

Clearly the reasons or grounds on which one is required to register are very important to the deontological model. One recent congressional rationale for FARA's requirement was that when lawmakers knew who was representing foreign interests they could better judge the information supplied by those representatives. This concern is about the effect that the carrier (the means of information or message transfer) has on the content of information supplied to the government. For example, information may be thought by those receiving it to be more or less valuable, depending upon the source or who brings the information. If, on the other hand, the FARA's continued enforcement is motivated by concern for the presumed harmful content of information itself, which is strictly a weighing of message content without concern for the context of the source or who brought the message (the means of transfer), then that motive must be weighed for rightness or wrongness by the deontologist.

Ultimately, the FARA indirectly limits the content of information available to U.S. citizens because those ideas carried by representatives of foreign entities are inhibited by a labyrinth of federal registration requirements. The problems of appropriately weighing the inhibitors information content versus restrictions for information carriers is a problem expressed by Congress but never adequately resolved, by their own admission. As recently as 1993, Congress continued to try to moderate the language of FARA so as to dilute the perception that foreign ideas are somehow less welcome in the United States.[20] The fact that Congress recognized and tried to act to mitigate the perception of content control suggests that there may be truth behind the notion that the law intends to prohibit foreign speech selectively.

Computer Security Act of 1987

The Computer Security Act protects 'sensitive information' contained in federal computer systems. The guidelines for protection are, according to the act, to be designed by an advisory committee that reports to Congress annually. Protection here is to be implemented by limiting the access to information which is designated as sensitive. Sensitive information, however, is ill-defined among agencies storing information in computer databases.

The Computer Security Act could be thought of as a law that limits access to government-held information. Strictly speaking, this kind of protection or control merely limits and does not prohibit access. But while nearly three million people held some level of security clearance in 1990,[21] many millions more did not have direct access to government-held information in these computer databases. The reasons for such protection or control offered by the executive branch during congressional hearings suggested an overarching concern for individual privacy and for national security against disgruntled employees that only the government could monitor appropriately.[22]

Here it is subtly assumed that government monitors itself best, and that information can be protected by controlling the people who have access to it. This kind of rationale speaks mostly closely to deontological theories, allowing that employees are obliged to act only in those ways prescribed by their employer. And that the employer—in this case, the executive branch of the government—has only good motives for prescribing certain rules of behavior, against which an employee must not act.

This kind of rationale also suggests that though the immediate consequence of the Computer Security Act is to limit information access to the security clearance community, the motive for instituting such limitations on the rest of the U.S. community outweighs what might be perceived as a cause for general unhappiness about limited access to information about government held by government. The executive branch conceded during congressional hearings that the private sector using these databases might be inconvenienced and excluded from some computer databases, but that the overriding concern ought to be the vulnerability of computer databases to "misuse, penetration or manipulation by disgruntled employees, terrorists, or others with criminal intent."[23] This justification seems to speak to the common good over the needs of individuals, but does not describe which common good nor who benefits.

The motive for information control, through restriction of information access, by the government is provided in order to outweigh the congressional concerns expressed as "the benefits of a full and open society exchang[ing] ideas and knowledge unfettered by governmental intervention and red tape."[24] In this case, deontologists might weigh the rightness or wrongness of motives and obligations of the government to protect privacy and national security, while teleologists might weigh the general happiness or unhappiness that is the consequence of limited information access in a community grounded in the free exchange of information.

Ultimately, Congress recognized that controlling the information carrier, in this case the computer database and computer technician, was a way of indirectly controlling information content. Much of the motivation for removing control from the executive branch by the statutory Computer Security Act was expressed in a House subcommittee report. "It would be impossible for the [Defense] department to strike an objective balance between the need to safeguard information and the need to maintain the free exchange of information."[25] The issue of controlling information content by the use of a classification category 'sensitive' which is outside the traditional security categories was still under congressional consideration as recently as 1994.[26]

Pentagon Media Rules

Some members of Congress expressed concern and dismay at the exclusion of media representatives during some phases of U.S. military action in Grenada and Panama. Their complaint was not about the exclusion of media representatives as much as about the limited access to timely information that was the consequence of the Pentagon's rules.[27] Repeatedly, congressional members cited the need for a free and open society in order that all necessary information be available to decision makers.[28]

The concerns expressed by both the executive branch and the legislators were for the general welfare of the country. As pivotal concerns, the executive branch cited their need to maintain national security and the legislators cited their need to be well informed before making decisions. Both sides seemed to assume and maintain the view that they—whichever "they" was speaking—knew better than any other "they" what was best for the country.[29]

Little concern was given to the limited information that the media pool provided to the rest of the country at a time when the country was not in political crisis or struggling against an on-shore and immediately threatening foe. The teleological perspective of possibly bad consequences for the general happiness if and when the general population has limited information about the situation was never a forefront issue.[30] Sporadically, the military claimed that limiting reporter access to military action was really a means of protecting the reporter from harm.[31] This claim might be taken as a teleological concern with an individual's happiness. The claim was rather quietly dismissed, however, as reporters pointed to the many previous military conflicts in which they had survived under their own care.[32]

Eventually both the executive and legislative branches recognized that by controlling the conduit/carrier access to information, the content of the information provided to the U.S. citizens was controlled as well. The military strategists were candid about what they saw as a benefit—information content controlled by way of access—of the Pentagon Media Rules. Congress, however, did not so much embrace the strategy but rather side-stepped the content issue that could have been taken up on behalf of the U.S. citizen; instead, Congress spoke in terms of congressional needs for information content that was reliable, if not unlimited.

CONCLUSIONS

The general question that begs to be answered is, What is the right thing to do in conflicts between information access and information control? There are a number of components, however, within that single question that need to be addressed before an adequate answer can be realized. One component involves separating ethical questions from the legal or practical. Another involves separating various ethical considerations that are likely to be found relevant. Conflicts in duties and conflicts in consequent benefit are two such considerations, and the ability to sort through them in an orderly fashion will aid in seeing clearly answers to the ethical questions broadly conceived and specifically encountered.

Clearly the government actions scrutinized here—the Foreign Agents Registration Act, the Computer Security Act and the Pentagon Media Rules, are legal acts. As they are legal acts, the government has both a right and a responsibility to enforce them. But the overarching question remains: Are these laws the right thing to do under the principles on which the U.S. government was founded? And apparently, that question is not so easily and clearly answered. It is this last question that is taken up in Chapter 7.

The laws cited as examples have been reviewed in some detail in previous chapters. First Amendment theories and ethical principles have been briefly reviewed, and the possible rationale provided in congressional debate briefly examined. Chapter 7 examines the parameters of information control specifically addressed by the federal regulations in the Foreign Agents Registration Act, the Computer Security Act and the Pentagon Media Rules in terms of the concerns about regulating information conduit/carrier as separate from information content. These specific issues of information control, within the context of underlying ethical principles, will be compared to those ethical principles evident in the federal government's primary documents, the Declaration of Independence and United States Constitution.

NOTES

1. For a further discussion, see Herbert Brucker, *Freedom of Information* (New York: Macmillan Co., 1949); James Russell Wiggins, *Freedom or Secrecy?* (New York: Oxford University Press, 1956); Benno C. Schmidt, Jr., *Freedom of the Press vs. Public Access* (New York: Praeger Publishers, 1976); Bill F. Chamberlin and Charlene J. Brown, eds., *The First Amendment Reconsidered* (New York: Longman, 1982).

2. Fred W. Friendly used this quote often in discussions of media ethics, and attributed it to Justice Potter Stewart. See Lisa H. Newton, *Ethics in America: Study Guide* (Englewood Cliffs, N.J.: Prentice-Hall Press, 1989) p.ix.

3. A Bill to Amend the Federal Election Campaign Act of 1971 to Provide

for a Voluntary System of Spending Limits and Partial Public Financing of Senate Primary and General Election Campaigns, and to Limit Contributions by Multicandidate Political Committees, and for Other Purposes, S. 87, 103d Cong., 1st Sess. (1993); A Bill to Restore Public Confidence in the Performance and Merits of Elected Officials and Federal Employees, S. 79, 103d Cong., 1st Sess. (1993); A Resolution to Amend the Rules of the House of Representatives to Establish a Citizens' Commission on Congressional Ethics, and for Other Purposes, H.Res. 43, 103d Cong., 1st Sess. (1993); A Bill to Amend the Federal Election Campaign Act of 1971 and Related Provisions of Law to Provide for a Voluntary System of Spending Limits and Benefits for House of Representatives Election Campaigns, and for Other Purposes, H.R. 275, 103d Cong., 1st Sess. (1993).

   4. Clifford Christians, Kim Rotzoll and Mark Fackler, *Media Ethics*, 3rd ed. (New York: Longman, 1991); H. Eugene Goodwin, *Groping for Ethics in Journalism* 2nd ed. (Ames: Iowa State University Press, 1987); Bruce M. Swain *Reporters' Ethics*, (Ames: Iowa State University Press, 1978).

   5. For example, see Bruce M. Swain, *Reporters' Ethics* (Ames: Iowa State University Press, 1978), ch.2, "Relationships with Sources"; ch.3, "Management Conflicts of Interest"; ch.4, "On and Off the Record"; ch.5, "Privacy"; ch.7, "Personal and Corporate Codes"; and appendix; H. Eugene Goodwin, *Groping for Ethics in Journalism* 2nd ed. (Ames: Iowa State University Press, 1987) ch.1, "The Search for Standards," and appendix; Clifford Christians, Kim Rotzoll and Mark Fackler, *Media Ethics*, 3rd ed. (New York: Longman, 1991) introduction.

   6. See David Vergobbi, "When Journalist Becomes Source: Excavating the Moral Dilemma of News-Rescue," paper presented at Association for Educations in Journalism and Mass Communication conference, August 1991, Boston, Mass.

   7. For further information and references on ethical theories, see appropriate entries in Paul Edwards, ed., *The Encyclopedia of Philosophy* (New York: Macmillan Publishing, 1967); Christina Hoff Sommers, *Right and Wrong: Basic Readings in Ethics* (New York: Harcourt Brace Jovanovich, 1986); William K. Frankena, *Ethics*, 2nd ed. (Englewood Cliffs, N.J.: Prentice Hall, 1973).

   8. Ruth Walden, "A Government Action Approach to First Amendment Analysis," *Journalism Quarterly* 69: 65-88 (Spring, 1992).

   9. Alexander Meiklejohn, *Free Speech and Its Relation to Self-Government* (New York: Harper, 1948).

   10. Thomas Emerson, "Toward a General Theory of the First Amendment," *Yale L.J.* 72: 877 (1963).

   11. Ronald Cass, "The Perils of Positive Thinking: Constitutional Interpretation and Negative First Amendment Theory," *UCLA L.Rev.* 34: 1405 (1987).

   12. Frederick Schauer, *Free Speech: A Philosophical Enquiry* (New York: Cambridge University Press, 1982).

13. For example, see Ralph Holsinger, *Media Law* (New York: Random House, 1987) 27.

14. Vincent Blasi, "The Checking Value in First Amendment Theory," *American Bar Foundation Research Journal* 1977: 523.

15. See *Black's Law Dictionary*, 5th ed. (St. Paul, Minn: West, 1983).

16. Schauer, *Free Speech*, 86.

17. Cass, 1479.

18. 22 U.S.C. §611.

19. See, for example, 22 *U.S.C.* §612 Registration statement, §614 Filing and labeling of political propaganda, §615 Books and records.

20. S. 90 Sec. 606, 103d Cong., 1st Sess. (1993); H.R. 823 Sec. 12, 103d Cong., 1st Sess. (1993).

21. S. 167 Sec. 202(c), 103d Cong., 1st Sess. (1993).

22. *Computer Security Research and Training Act of 1985: Hearings Before a Subcomm. of the H.R. Comm. on Government Operations*, 99th Cong., 1st Sess. (Sept. 18, 1985).

23. *Computer Security Research and Training Act of 1985: Hearings Before a Subcomm. of the H.R. Comm. on Government Operations*, 99th Cong., 1st Sess., (1985) 9.

24. H.R. Rep.No. 753, 99th Cong., 2d Sess. (1986), at pt.2, 9.

25. H.R. Rep.No. 753, 99th Cong., 2d Sess. (1986), at pt.2, 9.

26. S. 167 referred to the Senate Committee on Governmental Affairs, 103d Cong., 1st Sess. (1993).

27. *Hearings Before the Subcomm. on Courts, Civil Liberties and the Administration of Justice of the House Comm. on the Judiciary*, 98th Cong., 2d Sess. 3(1983); 134 *Cong. Rec.* S2440 (1988); *Cong. Rec.* E1442 (May 9, 1990); H.R.Rep. No. 102-5 Part 2, 102d Cong., 1st Sess. (1990).

28. See, for example, *The Persian Gulf Crisis: Joint Hearings Before the Subcomms. on Arms Control, International Security and Science, Europe and the Middle East, and on International Operations of the House Comm. on Foreign Affairs and the Joint Economic Comm.*, 101st Cong., 2d Sess. (1990).

29. See, for example, *Crisis in the Persian Gulf Region: U.S. Policy Options and Implications: Hearings Before the Senate Comm. on Armed Services*, 101st Cong., 2d Sess. (1990); *Crisis in the Persian Gulf: Sanctions, Diplomacy and War: Hearings Before the H.R. Comm. on Armed Services*, 101st Cong., 2d Sess. (1990).

30. See, for example, the opening statements, *Pentagon Rules on Media Access to the Persian Gulf War: Hearings Before the Senate Comm. on Governmental Affairs*, 102d Cong., 1st Sess. (1991).

31. See *Pentagon Media Ground Rules and Guidelines* (appendix C).

32. *Pentagon Rules Hearings*, 15.

Chapter 7

Ethical Principles in Federal Information Control

INTRODUCTION

Federally imposed controls on information flow may be justified in a number of ways to the satisfaction of a variety of moralists. This chapter details specifically the kinds of reasons legislators gave for allowing information controls such as the Foreign Agents Registration Act, the Computer Security Act and the Pentagon Media Rules. Their reasons are summarized in terms of the two general kinds of ethical theories described in Chapter 6—deontological and teleological—in order to build a framework that might be compared to the ethical principles of the founding framers of the U.S. Constitution.

NATURAL RIGHTS

In *The Federalist*, James Madison asserted, under the nom de plume "Publius," that the primary goal of good government is the safety and happiness of the governed.[1] The citizens are happiest, Publius wrote, when their natural rights are protected and exercised. Subsequently it has been suggested by philosophers and theorists that natural rights include the right to information that will enable individuals to make appropriate decisions about their lives and government.[2] The framers of the U.S. Constitution and The Bill of Rights may have believed this as well, and that is why they wrote the First Amendment's proviso that Congress shall make no laws that would restrict information flow through speech and print—the only means of mass communication known to the late 18th century founders.[3]

The notion of natural rights as a means of shaping government comes out of a deontological perspective, though the specific language might seem to be teleological talk about benefits with its references to happiness. The authors of the Constitution hinted, however, that these natural rights are bestowed by a Creator, and so mere mortals may not justly abridge them.[4] Natural rights are believed, then, to be inherent rights, not dependent on contractual agreement or the bestowal by government, or on the consequential results of their exercise. The talk of inherent rights makes the principles of the newly framed government fundamentally deontological, despite the talk of pursuit of happiness.[5] The Declaration of Independence, for example, described such rights as "unalienable" and Madison believed that they were so widely known, so inherent in the social character of human beings, that no statement of them was necessary in the federation's constitution.[6] Others, however, urged that this was not so, and the Bill of Rights was then written as a statement of these inherent rights.

THE FIRST AMENDMENT, DEONTOLOGY AND TELEOLOGY REVISITED

The First Amendment restrains Congress from making laws that restrict free speech or the press. One way to characterize speech and press in an 18th century frame is to recognize them as means of carrying ideas or information, and as the only practical means of mass communication in that day. Speech and press might also be thought to be maximally content-flexible—that is, any idea or set of information known at that time could be maximally distributed in either a speech or a press carrier.

Many theorists have asserted that the First Amendment was intended to protect a citizen's right to choose among ideas and information.[7] The rationale for this right to choose from a variety of ideas and information, particularly in a representative democracy, has in fact a long history.[8] More recently, however, the reasoning supporting this right to choose suggests that since the First Amendment explicitly protects information conduits or carriers (speech and press) it therefore implicitly protects content variety. One of the points that make this idea plausible is that the carriers explicitly protected in the First Amendment are maximally content-flexible, and so protection of them is implicitly protection of content flexibility.[9]

By late in the 19th century John Stuart Mill had popularized utilitarianism as a teleological perspective and as a driving moral principle for government.[10] But it was not until the early 20th century that the Supreme Court felt a need to begin sorting out the nation's emerging confusion about rationales supporting or limiting the First Amendment protections in the area of public policy. With established norms of natural rights based on deontological principles and emerging popular norms based on teleological principles, many lawmakers found it hard to resist the mingling of the principles that seemed to protect the nation.

Other protections found in legal language include protection of the nation, protection of the government and protection of the safety, welfare and happiness of citizens. While all of these use similar language, the concerns driving the protections are fundamentally different. For instance, protection of the nation is a concern for self-preservation of a society—the very life of it—and is thus a natural right; its concern is deontological. Promotion of welfare and happiness, on the other hand, is concerned with the quality and character of a life already assured; it is, therefore, a concern with consequences and is teleological in nature. This distinction might be seen as the difference between protecting society's life (deontological) and protecting society's life-style (teleological).

In a 1919 majority opinion, Justice Oliver Wendell Holmes asserted, "The most stringent protection of free speech would not protect a man in falsely shouting fire in a theatre and causing panic."[11] Holmes suggested a clear and present danger test for measuring the kinds of restrictions allowed on speech content relative to the result or consequences of the speech. Holmes' concern here was not simply with the preservation of life, but also with the preservation of a certain kind of order. One of the social worries at this time, for example, was over the economic and social disorder that labor unionization might cause. His concern for the result of the speech as a way of determining goodness or badness of the speech act is a teleological concern. The clear and present danger test suggests a shift away from deontological concerns for natural rights and duties toward concerns for consequences as a driving principle.

As the reasoning around First Amendment cases began to swing back and forth during the 1920s, one of the strongest statements made by Holmes might be read as an attempt to mingle deontological and teleological concerns under a single principle. These concerns were first deontological, that is, concerned with life preservation, and focused on the intentions of the speaker and not the particular speech content. And then they were teleological, that is, concerned with life-style, and looking at the results or consequences of the speech. In his 1925 dissenting opinion[12] Justice Holmes wrote, "Every idea is an incitement. It offers itself for belief and if believed it is acted on unless some other belief outweighs it. . . . The only difference between the expression of an opinion and an incitement in the narrower sense is the speaker's enthusiasm for the result." In the next paragraph, however, Holmes justifies his opinion in these terms. "The object would have been one with which the law might deal, subject to the doubt whether there was any danger that the publication could produce any result, or in other words, whether it was not futile and too remote from possible consequences."

This mixing not only affects early court decisions on First Amendment issues, under which the three federal actions discussed in the previous chapters might fall, but continues through the mid-century era of the more liberal Warren Court.[13] And this mixing of principles guiding First Amendment decisions was not confined to members of the Supreme Court. In a 1971 case[14] the solicitor general suggested to the justices that "the First Amendment was not intended to make it impossible for the executive branch to function or to protect the security of the United States." These concerns are on the one hand teleological—that is, for the bad results of dysfunctional government—and on the other hand deontological—that is, for the duty of government to protect the state. Justice Hugo Black's justification in defense of *The New York Times*, *Washington Post* and First Amendment is also split. First he cited a teleological concern with the results of a free press, and second he cited a deontological concern with the duties of the press. He wrote, "Only a free and unrestrained press can effectively expose deception in government. And paramount among the responsibilities of a free press is the duty to prevent any part of the government from deceiving the people."

More recently, and directly related to the specific examples of the previous chapters, is the 1987 opinion delivered by Justice John Paul Stevens III, about the intentions of the Foreign Agents Registration Act of 1938.[15] He wrote, "The statute does not prohibit the appellee from advising his audience."[16] This might be characterized as a teleological concern with consequence, in contrast to the deontological concern of congressional intentions surrounding FARA described by Justice Harry

A. Blackmun. Blackmun wrote, "The legislative history of the Act indicates that Congress fully intended to discourage communication by foreign agents."[17] He goes on by pointing to outcomes or results, a teleological perspective. The Court's error on neutrality of FARA's language leads it, he said, to ignore the practical effects of the classification contained in FARA.

THE LEGISLATURE

With at least seventy years of mixed reasons offered by the Supreme Court supporting, limiting and redefining the First Amendment, there can be little surprise at an equal amount of mixed driving principles voiced among congressional debaters on the issues of information control. It is this mixing which must be addressed now more fully. One way to go about this is by surveying the kinds of reasons given by congressional members for the recent information flow controls described in Chapters 3, 4 and 5. These reasons given in the context of each federal action are reviewed in the chronological order in which they were voiced and are divided among deontological concerns for natural rights and teleological concerns for consequences.

Controls over information content, however, ought not be found among the deontological perspectives,[18] but might be found among teleological perspectives dominated by concerns for immediate consequences. In keeping with the founding framers' First Amendment assumptions about stable, hands-off government and an informed electorate, it is reasonable to expect, as well, that conduit/carrier controls might be excluded from deontological perspectives. Deontological principles would probably, at best, tolerate information flow controls that preserve the government temporarily and only during times of extreme duress or direct life-threatening attack.

Foreign Agents Registration Act of 1938

The declarative amendment contained in the FARA said that the law is intended to "protect the national defense, internal security and foreign relations of the United States . . . so that government and the people of the United States may be informed of the identity of [foreign] persons and may appraise their statements and actions in light of their associations and activities."[19] FARA was intended, it might be inferred, to protect the United States as a nation, cited separately as government and people, from outside influences. These influences are identified here in the form of information provided to the U.S. public and the government. The declarative statement in FARA does not contain references to protection of natural rights for individuals, but rather to protection against bad consequences—government or people influenced by information provided by outsiders. The statute can be characterized, therefore, as intending to protect life-style.

A driving concern for consequences is a teleological norm, and it can be inferred here that the FARA is driven by teleological principles, so that the result or consequence justifies the means of achievement. Given the history of teleological principles evolving throughout the early 20th century it is no surprise that the FARA might be driven by such teleological principles. It is also important to note that the focus of the statute was not particularly on the speech content but on the speech source and carrier. Even at this time, the legislature understood that legal language directed at speech content might receive unsympathetic scrutiny by the courts.

Recent justifications for changes to the FARA include Representative Robert Kastenmeier's statement. "We live in a world that transcends borders. The sharing of ideas and information across international boundaries is imperative if we are to retain our competitive advantage. . . . America must set a clear and continuing example to the many other countries struggling to open their hearts and minds."[20] His concerns here are first with the consequences of shared ideas and information, and next with the duty that America has to set an example among nations. These are mixed teleological and deontological concerns. They are concerned first with prospering as a nation and second with responsibilities shouldered by stronger societies for weaker societies.

Legal counsel Peter Levine also suggested that the necessity of selective review prompted by the sheer volume of paperwork resulting from the FARA "raises serious questions as to how well FARA is serving its intended purpose of identifying the representatives of foreign interests in the United States and disclosing their activities."[21] This concern is clearly with the consequences of FARA's administration as it impedes or undermines FARA's intended purpose. The teleological thrust of the need for change here is simple and straight forward.

Questions continue to be raised about the appropriateness of legislation that separates foreigners and their representatives from U.S.

citizens. Representative Frank J. Guarini suggested that influences on the development of national policy by those who represent foreigners or interests outside the nation ought to be as much a concern now as they were during the 1930s. "Foreign influence continues to be exercised, for the most part in secret."[22] His support of changes to the FARA, he said, was to ensure against misinformation and misrepresentation. His concern here, then, might be characterized as that of the protection of life-style—teleological—rather than specifically with the protection of life.

Generally, then, concerns about protection of life-style and consequences, rather than concerns about protection of natural rights or duties, seem to dominate the history of the Foreign Agents Registration Act. Throughout the history, however, there was some attention given the presumption that information carrier/conduit aspects could be justifiably controlled through legislation, while information content was not explicitly and directly controlled.

Computer Security Act of 1987

The impetus for the Computer Security Act was explicitly a concern for security against, or protection from, the acts of questionable users. Assistant Secretary of Defense Donald Latham said in a May 27, 1986, *Washington Post* article, "I'm very concerned about what people are doing, and not just the Soviets. If that means putting a monitor on [computer] type systems, I'm for it." The concern here is results-driven justification for computer security. This is, of course, a teleological concern.

As noted in Chapter 4, the Department of Defense NSDD-145 contains a justification for additional computer security: that computers are vulnerable to "misuses, penetration or manipulation by disgruntled employees, terrorists, or others with criminal intent." Such misuses, one would have thought, may be life-style-threatening, but are not in general life-threatening, and so the concern here is, again, teleological.

In the "Poindexter Directive," also described in Chapter 4, 'sensitive information' is defined as "information the disclosure, loss, misuse, alteration, or destruction of which could adversely affect national security or other Federal Government interests." The justification here, it seems, is to develop a new classification of information outside the traditional system in place. The traditional system is generally accepted as a protection of information that is vital to the security of the nation in a narrow sense, that is, threats to the life of the nation.[23] The "Poindexter Directive," in contrast, is concerned with uses of information, and uses which adversely affect any or all government interests. This suggests that 'national security' in this context is thought of broadly as anything contributing to preservation of lifestyle, and so is a teleological concern.

In its final form, the CSA included in its definition of 'sensitive information,' any information "which could adversely affect . . . the privacy to which individuals are entitled" under the Privacy Act. This additional justification could be interpreted as concern for the citizens' natural rights of privacy, and thus be deontological.

Opponents of the bill suggested a deontological rationale against passage. American Civil Liberties Union chief legislative counsel Jerry Berman told the committee that he was worried that the bill would impede "the free flow of information, the public's right to know, the First Amendment values, including the right of citizens to be free of unwarranted intelligence surveillance."[24] This can be seen as a concern with natural rights, those enumerated in the Bill of Rights, for example.

The language of the statute explicitly addresses concerns of information content control by strictly prohibiting FOIA infractions. Even so, the implicit result of conduit or carrier controls is the control of information content classified as 'sensitive.' So although the statute attempts to avoid content control by placing restrictions only on the carrier, the use of the classification of 'sensitive' in conjunction with carrier restrictions has the net result of placing restrictions on information flow.

Pentagon Media Rules

Some justification for the Pentagon rules is to be found in the Ground Rules established by the Department of Defense in April 1990. Here it is suggested that the Rules "protect the security of the operation and the safety of the troops." The Ground Rules published in January 1991 directed that information should not be broadcast or published "because [doing so] could jeopardize operations and endanger lives."

It is not clear whose lives might be jeopardized, those of U.S. soldiers, U.S. citizens or civilians of the off-shore country. And since these rules applied to reporting of military operations on foreign soil involving what could be thought of as foreign internal matters in Grenada, Panama, and Kuwait, it is easy to see the military operations there as aimed at protecting American life-style rather than the very life of the U.S. nation. If, on the other hand, the internal situations in Grenada, Panama, or Kuwait are thought of as directly threatening the very life of the American government, then this justification might be seen as deontological in nature.

As reported in Chapter 5, testimony from the Central Command headquarters in August 1990 argued for the Pentagon Media Rules by asserting that "the enemy . . . can be expected [to plant] inaccurate data with selected media representatives or organizations . . . to adversely influence public opinion." Only in the most nationally-life-threatening kind of conflict could this defense be seen to be other than teleological.

Retired U.S. Army Col. Harry G. Summers, Jr., opposed the Pentagon Media Rules on the grounds that they "create the erroneous impression that the military has something to hide."[25] This is clearly a teleological objection, concerned with public relations rather than natural rights. This objection might be characterized as intending to meet the Rules' proponents head on: consequences against consequences.

Other opponents of the Pentagon Media Rules cited the appearance of "unwarranted prior restraint on the abilities of the U.S. news media to report . . . unfolding events to the American public."[26] This suggests that the Pentagon Media Rules may inhibit the flow of information to the American public that is part of the natural rights of free choice that the First Amendment is concerned to protect. The objection, then, since it is concerned with natural rights rather than outcomes, is deontological in character.

The Pentagon Media Rules places explicit restrictions both on information content and on information carriers without regard to protection of First Amendment natural rights. Carriers are restricted by the approval process and by the kinds of reporting activities that are allowed. Content is restricted by, among other things, an explicit list of categories of information that "are not releasable."

CONCLUSIONS

This review of legislative activity around the Foreign Agents Registration Act, the Computer Security Act and the Pentagon Media

Rules during the most recent decade suggests that a mixing of ethical principles may be at work in the decisions that affect information flow in the United States. This chronological representation of the sorts of arguments offered in support of federal control of information flow suggests that there is also some mixing of the direction and fundamental principles at work. Some proponents of information control defend the limited information flow in teleological terms of beneficial consequences or outcomes for the nation. And some proponents defend the action in deontological terms of rights and responsibilities carried by this nation among its peers. Clearly there is no single ethical principle or outlook at work among the supporting arguments.

The review of founding documents for the organization of the U.S. government suggests an ethical principle most similar to a deontological frame protecting natural rights. There is evidence to suggest, however, some subsequent confusion created by the 20th century notions of preferring to maintain social order within a certain life-style, as proclaimed in Supreme Court dicta in First Amendment cases about the consequence of clear and present danger.

Coincidentally, the aspects of 'information' represented in concerns about carrier/conduit and as content are given little direct consideration throughout the history of federal government action in the arena of information flow. But the First Amendment's initial protection of information carriers as a means of protecting the more important information content could be seen as very forward thinking on the issue that only now is being recognized. The Constitution's framers were, apparently, taking a stand on the deontological principle of the inalienable right of citizens to information content by formally prohibiting congressional action against information carriers.

NOTES

1. *The Federalist* Nos. 43 and 45, January 1788, and No. 62, February 1788.

2. See Judith Lichtenberg (ed.), *Democracy and the Mass Media* (New York: Cambridge University Press, 1990).

3. Stan Le Roy Wilson (ed.) *Mass Media/Mass Culture* (New York: Random House, 1989) 24-30.

4. John Locke, *An Essay Concerning the True Original Extent and End of Civil Government* (1689) ch 2. Also see Morton White, *Philosophy, The Federalist and the Constitution* (New York: Oxford University Press, 1987) 193-208.

5. For a more complete discussion of this, see Mortimer J. Adler, *Understanding the Ideas and the Ideals of the Constitution* (New York: Macmillan Publishing, 1987).

6. Michael Kammen (ed.), *The Origins of the American Constitution* (New York: Penguin Books, 1986) 51-122.

7. See Chapters 1 and 6.

8. See, for example, Aristotle, *The Athenian Constitution*, trans. P.J. Rhodes (New York: Penguin Books, 1984), 7.3, 41.3, 43.4-44, 45.4, 61.2, 62.2; Sir Henry Sumner Maine, *Ancient Law* (New York: Dorset Press, 1861) 36-93.

9. For more discussion, see Jeffery A. Smith, *Printers and Press Freedom* (New York: Oxford University Press, 1988) and Leonard W. Levy, *Emergence of a Free Press* (New York: Oxford University Press, 1985).

10. John Stuart Mill, *Representative Government* (1861); *Utilitarianism* (1863).

11. *Schenck v. United States*, 249 U.S. 47, 39 S.Ct. 247, 63 L.Ed. 470 (1919).

12. *Gitlow v. New York*, 268 U.S. 652, 45 S.Ct. 625, 69 L.Ed. 1138 (1925).

13. See, for example, Melvin I. Urofsky, *A March of Liberty*, Vol. II (New York: Alfred A. Knopf, 1988) 800-826.

14. *New York Times v. United States*, 403 U.S. 713, 91 S.Ct. 2140, 29 L.Ed.2d 822 (1971).

15. *Meese v. Keene*, 481 U.S. 465, 107 S.Ct. 1862, 95 L.Ed.2d 415 (1987).

16. *Meese v. Keene*, 1871.

17. *Meese v. Keene*, 1874.

18. Deontological natural rights here refers to the Publius populists who distributed the rights equally among all citizens, rather than the monarchists who distributed natural rights in greater measure to the king.

19. 22 U.S.C. §611.

20. *Free Trade in Ideas: Hearings Before the Subcomm. on Courts, Intellectual Property, and the Administration of Justice, H.R. Comm. on the Judiciary*, 101st Cong., 1st Sess. (May 3 and 4, 1989).

21. *The Federal Lobbying Disclosure Laws: Hearings Before the Subcomm. on Oversight of Government Management of the Senate Comm. on Governmental Affairs*, 102d Cong., 1st Sess. (1991) 164.

22. *Modification of the Foreign Agents Registration Act of 1938: Hearing Before the Subcomm. on Administrative Law and Governmental Relations of the H.R. Comm. on the Judiciary*, 102d Cong., 1st Sess. (1991) 75.

23. See, for example, Executive Orders 10,290 (1951), 11,652 (1972), 12,065 (1978), 12,356 (1982).

24. *Military and Civilian Control of Computer Security Issues: Hearing Before the Legislation and National Security Subcomm. of the H.R. Comm. on Government Operations*, 101st Cong., 1st Sess. (1989), 61.

25. *Pentagon Rules on Media Access to the Persian Gulf War: Hearings Before the Senate Comm. on Governmental Affairs*, 102 Cong., 1st Sess. (1991) 56.

26. H.R. Res. 37, 102d Cong., 1st Sess. (1991).

Chapter 8

Federal Information Control
in a Technological Age

Three interwoven dichotomies appear and reappear in the dynamics of
U.S. information control: information content versus carrier, natural
rights versus utility, and executive branch versus legislature. The
three pieces of information control regulation considered here can be
viewed as case studies in the shifting tensions and interactions of these
dichotomies.

FOUNDING DOCUMENTS

The original rationale for the protection of information flow in the
United States involved a concern for natural rights, as expressed in the
Declaration of Independence and the U.S. Constitution. The sorts of
natural rights that the founders of the U.S. government discussed were
considered absolute—that is, they were never to be abridged. Consequently the language of the First Amendment is stark, direct, and
exceptionless: "Congress shall make no law." Also, the rights were
thought to be neither the result of a contract nor dependent on the
character of the outcomes of their being exercised. Both the origins of
these rights, and their continuation, were seen as independent of agreements, human relationships, and predictable endings. For more than a
century, the principles guiding the federal government's information
control were thus deontological, connected to this view of natural
rights.

But since the mature development and popularization of
utilitarianism at the end of the nineteenth century, there has been a

gradual turn from concern for natural and inviolable rights of expression to a concern for expected outcomes of citizens' exercising these rights. That is, the more central focus has come to be on the consequences, utility, benefits and harms of information flow. Evidence of this change in focus is found in court decisions and opinions, and in the kind of legal controls placed on information flow in the twentieth century. The Foreign Agents Registration Act, the Computer Security Act and the Pentagon Media Rules provide three important examples of the sorts of legal controls to which government has turned in this century. Motivation and defenses of these controls have been predominantly teleological in nature.

The tension between the historically important conception of natural rights and the more modern attention to outcome-based utility has accelerated with the rapid expansion of communication media and the increased speed of communication. Members of the federal government have increasingly looked for way to control the vast information flow, but also recognized the need to appear to support the traditional protections found in the First Amendment.

These protections, being motivated by the idea of absolute natural rights, were content-neutral in character. That is, they protected expression regardless of the nature of the content of the message. One early avenue used by the legislature was to place controls on certain information conduits or carriers that were thought to be somehow outside the country's best interests. This sort of control was not aimed overtly at content, and therefore appeared to meet the requirement of being content-neutral. This means of control deflected constitutional arguments for free access and flow because it could be seen as similar to the already accepted restrictions of time, place and manner prescribed in First Amendment case law.

FIRST AMENDMENT VALUES, CARRIERS, CONTENT

Long-held principles of government allow for a certain amount of self-protection. That is, it is recognized that the government may have some right to protect the existing form of government, and so the framers tried to provide avenues for peaceful change within the government structure. But a fundamental principle of a representative democracy is to ensure that the means of self-protection of the government's structures are not used simply as a way to curtail opposition to particular governmental actions. And it was this particular concern among the founding framers—the curtailing of voices opposed to particular governmental actions—that prompted the inclusion of the First Amendment among the Bill of Rights.

The First Amendment uses specific and direct language to protect some sorts of information carriers—the press, for instance. Early legal interpretation of the U.S. Constitution saw it as intending to protect all political expression—no matter its content—but also determined that some limitations on carriers were reasonable. Among the limitations found reasonable by the courts were restrictions on the time, place, and manner of expression if these restrictions served some important government interest and alternative means, or carriers, of expression existed. This kind of limitation was motivated by teleological concerns for considerations such as civil and economic order. These were viewed as other government interests, and the adjudication of competing legitimate interests was seen in terms of happy consequences.

Paradoxically, recent legislation in the form of the FARA, CSA, and Pentagon Media Rules has attempted to appear not to limit content by, instead, limiting to near extinction the very entity the First Amendment explicitly protects—certain kinds of carriers. All three legislative actions are directed at carriers of information—both person to person as well as technologically enhanced information communication. Again, at the time of the First Amendment's writing, speech and press represented both person to person and technologically enhanced communication of information.

FOREIGN AGENTS REGISTRATION ACT, COMPUTER SECURITY ACT, AND PENTAGON MEDIA RULES

The three federal actions discussed in the previous chapters explicitly control information conduits and carriers. The teleological justifications forwarded for these controls are generally of a sort that look to outcomes, and are consistent with the trend of court opinion over the last seventy years. These controls, although they are couched in terms of carrier controls, invariably lead to certain kinds of content restrictions. That is to say, though the controls are stated in terms of carriers, their effect is not one of content-neutrality. In consequence, they pose conflicts with the foundational principles of the First Amendment.

The FARA, CSA, and Pentagon Media Rules were initiated by the executive branch, rather than a congressional delegation. Perhaps these initiatives came from the executive branch rather than the legislature because the First Amendment explicitly limits Congress' power to restrict information flow, and does not explicitly address restrictions on the executive branch. Consequently, the executive branch has powers in this sphere that are denied Congress. These powers enter at the point of administration and enforcement of law, which are executive functions.

For example, the FARA restrictions and subsequent conflicts arise from the selective interpretation and enforcement of the law by the Justice Department. Similarly, the CSA is the result of an executive directive, and the statutory product is now administered through the executive branch, which directs information protection through the federal government's computer system. And the Pentagon Media Rules were written by the Department of Defense, which is an arm of the executive branch.

POWERS WITHIN GOVERNMENT AND INFORMATION CONTROL

In keeping with the balance of power established by the Constitution, each of these executive branch actions received congressional attention. This attention, in all three of these examples, resulted in some modifications of an executive branch proposal; but, in each case, substantive regulations were subsequently codified. Through this kind of congressional reactive consideration of executive branch proactive administration, Congress allowed the executive branch to take the initiative in making law governing information control.

Yet the U.S. government is designed with the burden of law *making* resting primarily with the legislature. There is good reason for this, and the reason is magnified in cases of law concerned with information flow—an informed electorate is fundamental to the effective operation of a representative democracy like that of the United States.

The U.S. Constitution gives to the executive branch the function of administering law; that is, it is to bring about results envisioned by the electorate and enacted by the legislature. It is natural, then, that the concerns of the executive branch are often focused on outcomes and results. When Congress' duties are taken up by the executive branch, the electorate is left out of the process of defining the parameters of law. Since the executive branch is often primarily concerned with outcome-based administration, then the sorts of administrative laws promulgated will naturally be conceived, defended, and justified with teleological reasoning. And it is within this realm that the information control policy and laws shift concerns from natural rights to utility. They shift concerns, too, from protecting the form of government to protecting the substance of its specific actions.

This shift, in the de facto making of law that governs information flow, from Congress to the executive branch has brought with it, then, a shift in attention from natural rights to utility. Congress was originally thought of as not wholly or simply concerned with results, outcomes and utility in the ways in which an administrative department must be. One reminder of this was the limitations placed on Congress by the Bill of Rights. This cluster of shifts then has begun to effect changes on information flow that are not necessarily in the best interest of the electorate but, rather, serve administrative expediency.

DICHOTOMIES, SOLUTIONS AND INFORMATION FLOW

We see, then, tensions and interrelationships of three dichotomies related to information control legislation: content versus carrier, natural rights versus utility, and executive branch versus legislature. In the realm of information, U.S. law has seen natural rights as tied to content rather than carrier. The Constitution prohibits Congress from making laws that infringe those natural rights, that is, infringe on flow of content. The executive branch does not live under the same restrictions as Congress in this arena, however, and is also inherently utility-driven. Consequently it may be expected that if law making duties are implicitly left to the executive branch, then there may be a resulting shift away from natural rights and toward utility. Given the traditions of First Amendment law, this shift has been somewhat obscured by the allowance of restrictions on time, place, and manner of carriers rather than content.

The collective result, however, is that information flow is impeded, and that the executive branch has been allowed to determine how and in what ways. This has reduced the kinds of checks and balances envisioned by the Constitution, leaving much of the determination of information control in the hands of a relatively small number of federal bureaucrats more interested in the success of government actions than in the preservation of government's principles and ideals. If, however, the legislature is interested in preserving fundamental natural rights of constituents and in ensuring a well-informed electorate, then legislators must take proactive steps toward shaping an information policy that suits a technological age. Such a policy must encompass both information content and carriers and be one that preserves the founding principles of constitutional government.

Appendix A

The Foreign Agents Registration and Propaganda Act

The Foreign Agents Registration and Propaganda Act (FARA)[1] is one of only two statutes dealing specifically with information emanating from foreign governments.[2] Originally enacted in 1938, FARA was amended in 1939, 1942, 1950, 1956, 1961, 1966 and 1970. Many of these amendments were responses to specific fears about what seemed to be imminent danger to the government and the nation.[3] World War II, the 1950s red scare and the Vietnam War sparked, in turn, all of the changes after initial implementation of the FARA, except the 1983 congressional review.[4]

The legal disputes about the Justice Department's interpretation of the FARA between 1966 and 1984 were most often over the interpretation of the FARA definition of "propaganda."[5] And eventually, Congress' remedy to the dispute was to allow the President to name those nationalities exempt from registration as foreigners for the purposes of this statute.[6] This shifted the burden of separating friend from foe out of the hands of Congress and into the hands of the executive branch.

FOREIGN AGENTS AND PROPAGANDA

Registration of Foreign Propagandists
611. Definitions

As used in and for the purposes of this Act—

(a) The term "person" includes an individual, partnership, association, corporation, organization, or any other combination of individuals;

(b) The term "foreign principal" includes—

(1) a government of a foreign country and a foreign political party;

(2) a person outside of the United States, unless it is established that such person is an individual and a citizen of and domiciled within the United States, or that such person is not an individual and is organized under or created by the laws of the United States or of any State or other place subject to the jurisdiction of the United States and has its principal place of business within the United States; and

(3) a partnership, association, corporation, organization, or other combination of persons organized under the laws of or having its principal place of business in a foreign country.

(c) Except as provided in subsection (d) hereof, the term "agent of a foreign principal" means

(1) any person who acts as an agent, representative, employee, or servant, or any person who acts in any other capacity at the order, request, or under the direction or control, of a foreign principal or of a person any of whose activities are directly or indirectly supervised, directed, controlled, financed, or subsidized in whole or in major part by a foreign principal, and who directly or through any other person

(i) engages within the United States in political activities for or in the interests of such foreign principal;

(ii) acts within the United States as a public relations counsel, publicity agent, information service employee or political consultant for or in the interests of such foreign principal;

(iii) within the United States solicits, collects, disburses, or dispenses contributions, loans, money, or other things of value for or in the interest of such foreign principal; or

(iv) within the United States represents the interests of such foreign principal before any agency or official of the Government of the United States; and

(2) any person who agrees, consents, assumes or purports to act as, or who is or holds himself out to be, whether or not pursuant to contractual relationship an agent of a foreign principal as defined in clause (1) of this subsection.

(d) The term "agent of a foreign principal" does not include any news or press service or association organized under the laws of the United States or of any State or other place subject to the jurisdiction of the United States, or any newspaper, magazine, periodical, or other publication for which there is on file with the United States Postal Service information in compliance with Section 3611 [3685] of Title 39, United States Code [39 USCS 3685], published in the United States, solely by virtue of any bona fide news or journalistic activities, including the solicitation or acceptance of advertisements, subscriptions, or other compensation therefore, so long as it is at least 80 per cent beneficially owned by, and its officers and directors, if any, are citizens of the United States, and such news or press service or association, newspaper, magazine, periodicals or other publication is not owned, directed, supervised controlled, subsidized, or financed, and none of its policies are determined by any foreign principal defined in section 1(b) hereof [subsec. (b) of the section], or by any agent of a foreign principal required to register under this Act;

(e) The term "government of a foreign country" includes any person or group of persons exercising sovereign de facto or de jure political jurisdiction over any country, other than the United States, or over any part of such country, and includes any subdivision of any such group and any group or agency to which such sovereign de facto or de jure authority or functions are directly or indirectly delegated. Such term shall include any faction or body of insurgents within a country assuming to exercise governmental authority whether such faction or body of insurgents has or has not been recognized by the United States;

(f) The term "foreign political party" includes any organization or any other combination of individuals in a country other than the United States, or any unit or branch thereof, having for an aim or purpose, or which is engaged in any activity devoted in whole or in part to, the establishment, administration, control, or acquisition of administration or control, of a government of a foreign country or a subdivision thereof, or the furtherance or influencing of the political or public interests, policies, or relations of a government of a foreign country or a subdivision thereof;

(g) The term "public relations counsel" includes any person who engages directly or indirectly in forming, advising or in any way representing a principal in any public relations matter pertaining to political or public interests, policies or relations of such principal;

(h) The term "publicity agent" includes any person who engages directly or indirectly in the publication or dissemination of oral, visual, graphic, written, or pictorial information or matter of any kind, including publication by means of advertising, books, periodicals, newspapers, lectures, broadcasts, motion pictures, or otherwise;

(i) The term "information service employee" includes any person who is engaged in furnishing, disseminating, or publishing accounts, descriptions, information, or data with respect to the political, industrial, employment, economic, social, cultural, or other benefits, advantages, facts, or conditions of any country other than the United States or of any government of a foreign country or of a foreign political party or of a partnership, association, corporation, organization or other combination of individuals organized under the laws of, or having its principal place of business in, a foreign country;

(j) The term "political propaganda" includes any oral, visual, graphic, written, pictorial or other communication or expression by any person (1) which is reasonably adapted to, or which the person disseminating same believes will, or which he intends to, prevail upon, indoctrinate, convert, induce, or in any other way influence a recipient or any section of the public within the United States with reference to the political or public interests, policies, or relations of a government of a foreign country or a foreign political party or with reference to the foreign policies of the United States or promote in the United States racial, religious, or social dissensions, or (2) which advocates, advises, instigates, or promotes any racial, social, political or religious disorder, civil riot, or other conflict involving the use of force or violence in any other American republic or the overthrow of any government or political subdivision of any other American republic by any means involving the use of force or violence. As used in this section 1(j) [this subsection] the term "disseminating" includes transmitting or causing to be transmitted in the United States mails or by any means or instrumentality of interstate or foreign commerce or offering or causing to be offered in the United States mails;

(k) The term "registration statement" means the registration statement required to be filed with the Attorney General under section 2(a) hereof [22 USCS 612(a)], and any supplements thereto required to be filed under section 2(b) hereof [22 USCS 612(b)], and includes all documents and papers required to be filed therewith or amendatory thereof or supplemental thereto, whether attached thereto or incorporated therein by reference;

(l) The term "American republic" includes any of the states which were signatory to the Final Act of the Second Meeting of the Ministers of Foreign Affairs of the American Republics at Havana, Cuba, July 30, 1940;

(m) The term "United States," when used in a geographical sense, includes the several States, the District of Columbia, the Territories, the Canal Zone, the insular possessions. [including the Philippines Islands,] and all other places now or hereafter subject to the civil or military jurisdiction of the United States;

(n) The term "prints" means newspapers and periodicals, books, pamphlets, sheet music, visiting cards, address cards, printing proofs, engravings, photographs, pictures, drawings, plans, maps, patterns to be cut out, catalogs, prospectuses, advertisements, and printed, engraved, lithographed, or autographed notices of various kinds, and, in general, all impressions or reproductions obtained on paper or other material assimilable to paper, on parchment or on cardboard, by means of printing, engraving, lithography, autography, or any other easily recognizable mechanical process, with the exception of the copying press, stamps with movable or immovable type, and the typewriter;

(o) The term "political activities" means the dissemination of political propaganda and any other activity which the person engaging therein believes will, or which he intends to, prevail upon, indoctrinate, convert, induce, persuade, or in any other way influence any agency or official of the government of the United States or any section of the public within the United States with reference to formulating, adopting, or changing the domestic or foreign policies of the United States or with reference to the political or public interests, policies, or relations of a government of a foreign country or a foreign political party;

(p) The term "political consultant" means any person who engages in informing or advising any other person with reference to the domestic or foreign policies of the United States or the political or public interest, policies, or relations of a foreign country or of a foreign political party;

(q) For the purpose of section (3)(d) hereof [22 USCS 613(d)], activities in furtherance of the bona fide commercial, industrial or financial interests of a domestic person engaged in substantial commercial, industrial or financial operations in the United States shall not be deemed to serve predominantly a foreign interest because such activities also benefit the interests of a foreign person engaged in bona fide trade or commerce which is owned or controlled by, or which owns or controls, such domestic person:

Provided, that

(i) such foreign person is not, and such activities are not directly or indirectly supervised, directed, controlled, financed or subsidized in whole or in substantial part by, a government of a foreign country or a foreign political party,

(ii) the identity of such foreign person is disclosed to the agency or official of the United States with whom such activities are conducted, and

(iii) whenever such foreign person owns or controls such domestic person, such activities are substantially in furtherance of the bona fide commercial, industrial or financial interests of such domestic person.

612. Registration statement

(a) Filing; contents. No person shall act as an agent of a foreign principal unless he has filed with the Attorney General a true and complete registration statement and supplements thereto as required by this section 2(a) and section 2(b) hereof [subsecs. (a) and (b) of this section] or unless he is exempt from registration under the provisions of this Act. Except as hereinafter provided, every person who becomes an agent of a foreign principal shall, within ten days thereafter, file with the Attorney General, in duplicate, a registration statement, under oath on a form prescribed by the Attorney General. The obligation of an agent of a foreign principal to file a registration statement shall, after the tenth day of his becoming such agent, continue from day to day, and termination of such status shall not relieve such agent from his obligation to file a registration statement for the period during which he was an agent of a foreign principal. The registration statement shall include the following, which shall be regarded as material for the purposes of this Act:

(1) Registrant's name, principal business address, and all other business addresses in the United States or elsewhere, and all residence addresses, if any;

(2) Status of the registrant; if an individual, nationality; if a partnership, name, residence addresses, and nationality of each partner and a true and complete copy of its articles of copartnership; if an association, corporation, organization, or any other combination of individuals, the name, residence addresses, and nationality of each director and officer and of

each person performing the functions of a director or officer and a true and complete copy of its charter, articles of incorporation, association, constitution, and bylaws, and amendments thereto; a copy of every other instrument or document and a statement of the terms and conditions of every oral agreement relating to its organization, powers, and purposes; and a statement of its ownership and control;

(3) A comprehensive statement of the nature of registrant's business; a complete list of registrant's employees and a statement of the nature of the work of each; the name and address of every foreign principal for whom the registrant is acting, assuming or purporting to act or has agreed to act; the character of the business or other activities of every such foreign principal, and, if any such foreign principal be other than a natural person, a statement of the ownership and control of each; and the extent, if any, to which each such foreign principal is supervised, directed, owned, controlled, financed, or subsidized, in whole or in part, by any government of a foreign country or foreign political party, or by any other foreign principal;

(4) Copies of each written agreement and the terms and conditions of each oral agreement, including all modifications of such agreements, or, where no contract exists, a full statement of all the circumstances, by reason of which the registrant is an agent of a foreign principal; a comprehensive statement of the nature and method of performance of each such contract, and of the existing and proposed activity or activities engaged in or to be engaged in by the registrant as agent of a foreign principal for each such foreign principal, including a detailed statement of any such activity which is a political activity;

(5) The nature and amount of contributions, income, money, or thing of value, if any, that the registrant has received within the preceding sixty days from each such foreign principal, either as compensation or for disbursement or otherwise, and the form and time of each such payment and from whom received;

(6) A detailed statement of every activity which the registrant is performing or is assuming or purporting or has agreed to perform for himself or any other person other than a foreign principal and which requires his registration hereunder;

(7) The name, business, and residence addresses, and if an individual, the nationality, of any person other than a foreign principal for whom the registrant is acting, assuming or purporting to act or has agreed to act under such circumstances as require his registration hereunder; the extent to which each such person is supervised, directed, owned, controlled, financed, or subsidized, in whole or in part, by any government of a foreign country or foreign political party or by any other foreign principal; and the nature and amount of contributions, income, money, or thing of value, if any, that the registrant has received during the preceding sixty days from each such person in connection with any of the activities referred to in clause (6) of this subsection, either as compensation or for disbursement or otherwise, and the form and time of each such payment and from whom received;

(8) A detailed statement of the money and other things of value spent or disposed of by the registrant during the preceding sixty days in furtherance of or in connection with activities which require his registration hereunder and which have been undertaken by him either as an agent of a foreign principal or for himself or any other person or in connection with any activities relating to his becoming an agent of such principal, and a detailed statement of any contributions of money or other things of value made by him during the preceding sixty days (other than contributions the making of which is prohibited under the terms of section 613 of title 18, United States Code) in connection with an election to any political office or in connection with any primary election, convention, or caucus held to select candidates for any political office;

(9) Copies of each written agreement and the terms and conditions of each oral agreement, including all modifications of such agreements, or, where no contract exists, a full statement of all the circumstances, by reason of which the registrant is performing or assuming or purporting or has agreed to perform for himself or for a foreign principal or for any person other than a foreign principal any activities which require his registration hereunder;

(10) Such other statements, information, or documents pertinent to the purposes of this Act as the Attorney General, having due regard for the national security and the public interest, may from time to time require;

(11) Such further statements and such further copies of documents as are necessary to make the statements made in the registration statement and supplements thereto, and the copies of documents furnished therewith, not misleading.

(b) Supplements; filing period. Every agent of a foreign principal who has filed a registration statement required by section 2(a) hereof [subsec. (a) of this section] shall, within thirty days after the expiration of each period of six months succeeding such filing, file with the Attorney General a supplement thereto, under oath, on a form prescribed by the Attorney General, which shall set forth with respect to such preceding six months' period such facts as the Attorney General, having due regard for the national security and the public interest, may deem necessary to make the information required under section 2 hereof [this section] accurate, complete, and current with respect to such period. In connection with the information furnished under clauses (3), (4), (6), and (9) of section 2(a) hereof [subsec. (a) (3), (4), (6), (9) of this section], the registrant shall give notice to the Attorney General of any changes therein within ten days after such changes occur. If the Attorney General, having due regard for the national security and the public interest, determines that it is necessary to carry out the purposes of this Act, he may, in any particular case, require supplements to the registration statement to be filed at more frequent intervals in respect to all or particular items of information to be furnished.

(c) Execution of statement under oath. The registration statement and supplement thereto shall be executed under oath as follows: If the registrant is an individual, by him; if the registrant is a partnership, by the majority of the members thereof; if the registrant is a person other than an individual or a partnership, by a majority of the officers thereof or persons performing the functions of officers or by a majority of the board of directors thereof or persons performing the functions of directors, if any.

(d) Filing of statement not deemed full compliance nor as preclusion from prosecution. The fact that a registration statement or supplement thereto has been filed shall not necessarily be deemed a full compliance with this Act and the regulations thereunder on the part of the registrant; nor shall it indicate that the Attorney General has in any way passed upon the merits of such registration statement or supplement thereto; nor shall it preclude prosecution, as provided for in this Act, for willful failure to file a registration statement or supplement thereto when due or for a willful false statement of a material fact therein or the willful omission of a material fact required to be stated therein or the willful omission of a material fact or copy of a material document necessary to make the statements made in a registration statement and supplements thereto, and the copies of documents furnished therewith, not misleading.

(e) Incorporation of previous statement by reference. If any agent of a foreign principal, required to register under the provisions of this Act, has previously thereto registered with the Attorney General under the provisions of the Act of October 17, 1940 (54 Stat. 1201), the Attorney General, in order to eliminate inappropriate duplication, may permit the incorporation by reference in the registration statement or supplements thereto filed hereunder of any information or documents previously filed by such agent of a foreign principal under the provisions of the Act of October 17, 1940 (54 Stat. 1201).

(f) Exemption by Attorney General. The Attorney General may, by regulation, provide for the exemption—

> (1) from registration, or from the requirement of furnishing any of the information required by this section, of any person who is listed as a partner, officer, director, or employee in the registration statement filed by an agent of a foreign principal under this Act, and
>
> (2) from the requirement of furnishing any of the information required by this section of any agent of a foreign principal, where by reason of the nature of the functions or activities of such person the Attorney General, having due regard for the national security and the public interest, determines that such registration, or the furnishing of such information, as the case may be, is not necessary to carry out the purposes of this Act.

613. Exemptions

The requirements of section 2(a) hereof [22 USCS @ 612(a)] shall not apply to the following agents of foreign principals:

(a) Diplomatic or consular officers. A duly accredited diplomatic or consular officer of a foreign government who is so recognized by the Department of State, while said officer is engaged exclusively in activities which are recognized by the Department of State as being within the scope of the functions of such officer;

(b) Official of foreign government. Any official of a foreign government, if such government is recognized by the United States, who is not a public-relations counsel, publicity agent, information-service employee, or a citizen of the United States, whose name and status and the character of whose duties as such official are of public record in the Department of State, while said official is engaged exclusively in activities which are recognized by the Department of State as being within the scope of the functions of such official;

(c) Staff members of diplomatic or consular officers. Any member of the staff of, or any person employed by, a duly accredited diplomatic or consular officer of a foreign government who is so recognized by the Department of State, other than a public-relations counsel, publicity agent, or information-service employee, whose name and status and the character of whose duties as such member or employee are of public record in the Department of State, while said member or employee is engaged exclusively in the performance of activities which are recognized by the Department of State as being within the scope of the functions of such member or employee;

(d) Private and nonpolitical activities; solicitation of funds. Any person engaging or agreeing to engage only (1) in private and nonpolitical activities in furtherance of the bona fide trade or commerce of such foreign principal; or (2) in other activities not serving predominantly a foreign interest; or (3) in the soliciting or collecting of funds and contributions within the United States to be used only for medical aid and assistance, or for food and clothing to relieve human suffering, if such solicitation or collection of funds and contributions is in accordance with and subject to the provisions of the Act of November 4, 1939, as amended (54 Stat. 4), and such rules and regulations as may be prescribed thereunder;

(e) Religious, scholastic, or scientific pursuits. Any person engaging or agreeing to engage only in activities in furtherance of bona fide religious, scholastic, academic, or scientific pursuits or of the fine arts;

(f) Defense of foreign government vital to United States defense. Any person, or employee of such person, whose foreign principal is a government of a foreign country the defense of which the President deems vital to the defense of the United States while, (1) such person or employee engages only in activities which are in furtherance of the policies, public interest, or national defense both of such government and of the Government of the United States, and are not intended to conflict with any of the domestic or foreign policies of the Government of the United States, (2) each communication or expression by such person or employee which he intends to, or has reason to believe will, be published, disseminated, or circulated among any section of the public, or portion thereof, within the United States, is a part of such activities and is believed by such person to be truthful and accurate and the identity of such person as an agent of such foreign principal is disclosed therein, and (3) such government of a foreign country furnishes to the Secretary of State for transmittal to, and retention for the duration of this Act by, the Attorney General such information as to the identity and activities of such person or employee at such times as the Attorney General may require. Upon notice to the Government of which such person is an agent or to such person or employee, the Attorney General, having due regard for the public interest and national defense, may, with the approval of the Secretary of State, and shall, at the request of the Secretary of State, terminate in whole or in part the exemption herein of any such person or employee;

(g) Persons qualified to practice law. Any person qualified to practice law, insofar as he engages or agrees to engage in the legal representation of a disclosed foreign principal before any court of law or any agency of the Government of the United States:

Provided, that for the purposes of this subsection legal representation does not include attempts to influence or persuade agency personnel or officials other than in the course of established agency proceedings, whether formal or informal

614. Filing and labeling of political propaganda

(a) Copies to Attorney General; statement as to places, times, and extent of transmission. Every person within the United States who is an agent of a foreign principal and required to register under the provisions of this Act and who transmits or causes to be transmitted in the United States mails or by any means or instrumentality of interstate or foreign commerce any political propaganda for or in the interests of such foreign principal (i) in the form of prints, or (ii) in any other form which is reasonably adapted to being, or which he believes will be, or which he intends to be, disseminated or circulated among two or more persons shall, not later than forty-eight hours after the beginning of the transmittal thereof, file with the Attorney General two copies thereof and a statement, duly signed by or on behalf of such agent, setting forth full information as to the places, times, and extent of such transmittal.

(b) Identification statement. It shall be unlawful for any person within the United States who is an agent of a foreign principal and required to register under the provisions of this Act to transmit or cause to be transmitted in the United States mails or by any means or instrumentality of interstate or foreign commerce any political propaganda for or in the interests of such foreign principal (i) in the form of prints, or (ii) in any other form which is reasonably adapted to being, or which he believes will be, or which he intends to be, disseminated or circulated among two or more persons, unless such political propaganda is conspicuously marked at its beginning with, or prefaced or accompanied by, a true and accurate statement, in the language or languages used in such political propaganda, setting forth the relationship or connection between the person transmitting the political propaganda or causing it to be transmitted and such propaganda; that the person transmitting such political propaganda or causing it to be transmitted is registered under this Act with the Department of Justice, Washington, District of Columbia, as an agent of a foreign principal, together with the name and address of such agent of a foreign principal and of such foreign principal; that, as required by this Act, his registration statement is available for inspection at and copies of such political propaganda are being filed with the Department of Justice; and that registration of agents of foreign principals required by the Act does not indicate approval by the United States Government of the contents of their political propaganda. The Attorney General, having due regard for the national security and the public interest, may by regulation prescribe the language or languages and the manner and form in which such statement shall be made and require the inclusion of such other information contained in the registration statement identifying such agent of a foreign principal and such political propaganda and its sources as may be appropriate.

(c) Public inspection. The copies of political propaganda required by this Act to be filed with the Attorney General shall be available for public inspection under such regulations as he may prescribe.

(d) Library of Congress. For purposes of the Library of Congress, other than for public distribution, the Secretary of the Treasury and the Postmaster General are authorized, upon the request of the Librarian of Congress, to forward to the Library of Congress fifty copies, or as many fewer thereof as are available, of all foreign prints determined to be prohibited entry under the provisions of section 305 of title III of the Act of June 17, 1930 (46 Stat. 688) [19 USCS @ 1305], and of all foreign prints excluded from the mails under authority of section 1 of title XII of the Act of June 15, 1917 (40 Stat. 230).

Notwithstanding the provisions of section 305 of title III of the Act of June 17, 1930 (46 Stat. 688) [19 USCS @ 1305], and of section 1 of title XII of the Act of June 15, 1917 (40 Stat. 230), the Secretary of the Treasury is authorized to permit the entry and the Postmaster General is authorized to permit the transmittal in the mails of foreign prints imported for governmental purposes by authority or for the use of the United States or for the use of the Library of Congress.

(e) Information furnished to agency or official of United States government. It shall be unlawful for any person within the United States who is an agent of a foreign principal required to register under the provisions of this Act to transmit, convey, or otherwise furnish to any agency or official of the Government (including a Member or committee of either House of Congress) for or in the interests of such foreign principal any political propaganda or to request from any such agency or official for or in the interests of such foreign principal any information or advice with respect to any matter pertaining to the political or public interests, policies or relations of a foreign country or of a political party or pertaining to the foreign or domestic policies of the United States unless the propaganda or the request is prefaced or accompanied by a true and accurate statement to the effect that such person is registered as an agent of such foreign principal under this Act.

(f) Appearances before Congressional committees. Whenever any agent of a foreign principal required to register under this Act appears before any committee of Congress to testify for or in the interests of such foreign principal, he shall, at the time of such appearance, furnish the committee with a copy of his most recent registration statement filed with the Department of Justice as an agent of such foreign principal for inclusion in the records of the committee as part of his testimony.

615. Books and records

Every agent of a foreign principal registered under this Act shall keep and preserve while he is an agent of a foreign principal such books of account and other records with respect to all his activities, the disclosure of which is required under the provisions of this Act, in accordance with such business and accounting practices, as the Attorney

General, having due regard for the national security and the public interest, may by regulation prescribe as necessary or appropriate for the enforcement of the provisions of this Act and shall preserve the same for a period of three years following the termination of such status. Until regulations are in effect under this section every agent of a foreign principal shall keep books of account and shall preserve all written records with respect to his activities. Such books and records shall be open at all reasonable times to the inspection of any official charged with the enforcement of this Act. It shall be unlawful for any person willfully to conceal, destroy, obliterate, mutilate, or falsify, or to attempt to conceal, destroy, obliterate, mutilate, or falsify, or to cause to be concealed, destroyed, obliterated, mutilated, or falsified, any books or records required to be kept under the provisions of this section.

616. Public examination of official records; transmittal of records and information

(a) Permanent copy of statement; inspection; withdrawal. The Attorney General shall retain in permanent form one copy of all registration statements and all statements concerning the distribution of political propaganda furnished under this Act, and the same shall be public records and open to public examination and inspection at such reasonable hours, under such regulations, as the Attorney General may prescribe, and copies of the same shall be furnished to every applicant at such reasonable fee as the Attorney General may prescribe. The Attorney General may withdraw from public examination the registration statement and other statements of any agent of a foreign principal whose activities have ceased to be of a character which requires registration under the provisions of this Act.

(b) Secretary of State. The Attorney General shall, promptly upon receipt, transmit one copy of every registration statement filed hereunder and one copy of every amendment or supplement thereto, and one copy of every item of political propaganda filed hereunder, to the Secretary of State for such comment and use as the Secretary of State may determine to be appropriate from the point of view of the foreign relations of the United States. Failure of the Attorney General so to transmit such copy shall not be a bar to prosecution under this Act.

(c) Executive departments and agencies; Congressional committees. The Attorney General is authorized to furnish to departments and agencies in the executive branch and committees of the Congress such information obtained by him in the administration of this Act, including the names of registrants under this Act, copies of registration statements, or parts thereof, copies of political propaganda, or other documents or information filed under this Act, as may be appropriate in the light of the purposes of this Act.

617. Liability of officers

Each officer, or person performing the functions of an officer, and each director, or person performing the functions of a director, of an agent of a foreign principal which is not an individual shall be under obligation to cause such agent to execute and file a registration statement and supplements thereto as and when such filing is required under section 2(a) and 2(b) hereof [22 USCS @ 612(a), (b)] and shall also be under obligation to cause such agent to comply with all the requirements of sections 4(a), 4(b), and 5 [22 USCS @ 614(a), (b), 615] and all other requirements of this Act. Dissolution of any organization acting as an agent of a foreign principal shall not relieve any officer, or person performing the functions of an officer, or any director, or person performing the functions of a director, from complying with the provisions of this section. In case of failure of any such agent of a foreign principal to comply with any of the requirements of this Act, each of its officers, or persons performing the functions of officers, and each of its directors, or persons performing the functions of directors, shall be subject to prosecution therefore.

618. Enforcement and penalties

(a) Violations; false statements and willful omissions. Any person who—

> (1) willfully violates any provision of this Act or any regulation thereunder, or
> (2) in any registration statement or supplement thereto or in any statement under section 4(a) hereof [22 USCS @ 614(a)] concerning the distribution of political propaganda or in any other document filed with or furnished to the Attorney General

under the provisions of this Act willfully makes a false statement of a material fact or willfully omits any material fact required to be stated therein or willfully omits a material fact or a copy of a material document necessary to make the statements therein and the copies of documents furnished therewith not misleading, shall, upon conviction thereof, be punished by a fine of not more than $10,000 or by imprisonment for not more than five years, or both, except that in the case of a violation of subsection (b), (e), or (f) of section 4 [22 USCS @ 614(b), (e), or (f)] or of subsection (g) or (h) of this section the punishment shall be a fine of not more than $ 5,000 or imprisonment for not more than six months, or both.

(b) Proof of identity of foreign principal. In any proceeding under this Act in which it is charged that a person is an agent of a foreign principal with respect to a foreign principal outside of the United States, proof of the specific identity of the foreign principal shall be permissible but not necessary.

(c) Deportation. Any alien who shall be convicted of a violation of, or a conspiracy to violate, any provision of this Act or any regulation thereunder shall be subject to deportation in the manner provided by sections 241, 242, and 243 of the Immigration and Nationality Act [8 USCS @ 1251—1253].

(d) Non Mailable matter. The Postmaster General may declare to be non mailable any communication or expression falling within clause (2) of section 1(j) hereof [22 USCS @ 611(j)(2)] in the form of prints or in any other form reasonably adapted to, or reasonably appearing to be intended for, dissemination or circulation among two or more persons, which is offered or caused to be offered for transmittal in the United States mails to any person or persons in any other American republic by any agent of a foreign principal, if the Postmaster General is informed in writing by the Secretary of State that the duly accredited diplomatic representative of such American republic has made written representation to the Department of State that the admission or circulation of such communication or expression in such American republic is prohibited by the laws thereof and has requested in writing that its transmittal thereto be stopped.

(e) Continuing offense. Failure to file any such registration statement or supplements thereto as is required by either section 2(a) or section 2(b) [22 USCS @ 612(a) or (b)] shall be considered a continuing offense for as long as such failure exists, notwithstanding any statute of limitation or other statute to the contrary.

(f) Injunctive remedy; jurisdiction of district court; expedition of proceedings. Whenever in the judgment of the Attorney General any person is engaged in or about to engage in any acts which constitute or will constitute a violation of any provision of this Act, or regulations issued thereunder, or whenever any agent of a foreign principal fails to comply with any of the provisions of this Act or the regulations issued thereunder, or otherwise is in violation of the Act, the Attorney General may make application to the appropriate United States district court for an order enjoining such acts or enjoining such person from continuing to act as an agent of such foreign principal, or for an order requiring compliance with any appropriate provision of the Act or regulation thereunder. The district court shall have jurisdiction and authority to issue a temporary or permanent injunction, restraining order or such other order which it may deem proper.

(g) Deficient registration statement. If the Attorney General determines that a registration statement does not comply with the requirements of this Act or the regulations issued thereunder, he shall so notify the registrant in writing, specifying in what respects the statement is deficient. It shall be unlawful for any person to act as an agent of a foreign principal at any time ten days or more after receipt of such notification without filing an amended registration statement in full compliance with the requirements of this Act and the regulations issued thereunder.

(h) Contingent fee arrangement. It shall be unlawful for any agent of a foreign principal required to register under this Act to be a party to any contract, agreement, or understanding, either express or implied, with such foreign principal pursuant to which the amount or payment of the compensation, fee, or other remuneration of such agent is contingent in whole or in part upon the success of any political activities carried on by such agent.

619. Territorial applicability of 22 USCS @ 611 et seq.

This Act shall be applicable in the several States, the District of Columbia, the Territories, the Canal Zone, the insular possessions, [including the Philippine Islands,] and all other places now or hereafter subject to the civil or military jurisdiction of the United States.

620. Rules and regulations

The Attorney General may at any time make, prescribe, amend, and rescind such rules, regulations, and forms as he may deem necessary to carry out the provisions of this Act.

NOTES

1. 22 U.S.C. §611-621 (1992).
2. 26 U.S.C. §501 and 504 require lobbying organizations to report their tax status.
3. See H.R. Rep. No. 198, 73rd Cong., 2d Sess. (1934) and 78 Cong. Rec. 13-14 (1934); H.R. Rep. No. 153, 74th Cong. 1st Sess. 23 (1935); H.R. Rep. No. 1381, 75th Cong. 1st Sess. 1-2 (1937); H.R. Doc. No. 611, 77th Cong. 2d Sess. 2 (1942); S.Rep. No. 1453, 89th Cong. 1st Sess. 3 (1965).
4. H.R. Rep. 36, 98th Cong., 1st Sess., (1983).
5. Cong. Research Service, 95th Cong., 1 Sess., *The Foreign Agents Registration Act* (Senate Foreign Relations Comm. Print 1977); also see Ava Marion Plakins, "Political Propaganda," *Fordham International Law Journal* 11: 185 (1987).
6. 22 U.S.C. §613(f).

Appendix B

The Computer Security Act of 1987

The *Computer Security Act* (CSA)[1] was passed by Congress after some debate[2] and signed eagerly into law by President Ronald Reagan.[3] The CSA empowers the government to design and implement a security system for data contained on software that is either generated by the government or purchased/leased by the government from non-government sources. For example, the government regularly contracts private computer firms to complete specific data processing projects, during which the private company is subject to the security system used by the government for as long as the government requires. Similarly, the federal government is a major source of funding for many universities' research programs, and the contracts attached to that money often require the researchers to adhere to information security standards designed by the government.[4]

This new security measure, the Computer Security Act, applies to all databases that contain "sensitive information." Sensitive information is a classification outside the security classification system traditionally used for government-held information—as used, for instance, in FOIA requests. The information guarded by the Computer Security Act for its sensitive nature would be available only to those employees with government clearance when this new law is broadly applied.

COMPUTER SECURITY ACT OF 1987

To provide for a computer standards program within the National Bureau of Standards, to provide for Government-wide computer security, and to provide for the training in security matters of persons who are involved in the management, operation, and use of Federal computer systems, and for other purposes.

Be it enacted by the Senate and House of Representatives of the United States of America in Congress assembled,

Section 1. Short Title.
This Act may be cited as the "Computer Security Act of 1987."

Sec. 2. Purpose.
(a) In General—The Congress declares that improving the security and privacy of sensitive information in Federal computer systems is in the public interest, and hereby creates a means for establishing minimum acceptable security practices for such systems, without limiting the scope of security measures already planned or in use.

(b) Specific Purposes—The purposes of this Act are

(1) by amending the Act of March 3, 1901, to assign to the National Bureau of Standards responsibility for developing standards and guidelines for Federal computer Systems, including responsibility for developing standards and guidelines needed to assure the cost-effective security and privacy of sensitive information in Federal computer systems, drawing on the technical advice and assistance (including work products) of the National Security Agency, where appropriate;

(2) to provide for promulgation of such standards and guidelines by amending section 111(d) of the Federal Property and Administrative Services Act of 1949;

(3) to require establishment of security plans by all operators of Federal computer systems that contain sensitive information; and

(4) to require mandatory periodic training for all persons involved in management, use, or operation of Federal computer systems that contain sensitive information.

Sec. 3. Establishment of Computer Standards Program.
The Act of March 3, 1901 (15 U.S.C. 271-278h), is amended—

(1) in section 2(f), by striking out "and" at the end of paragraph (18), by striking out the period at the end of paragraph (19) and insert-

ing in lieu thereof: "; and", and by inserting after such paragraph the following:

"(2) the study of computer systems (as that term is defined in section 20(d) of this Act) and their use to control machinery and processes.";

(2) by redesignating section 20 as section 22, and by inserting after section 19 the following new sections:

"Sec. 20. (a) The National Bureau of Standards shall—

"(1) have the mission of developing standards, guidelines, and associated methods and techniques for computer systems;

"(2) except as described in paragraph (3) of this subsection (relating to security standards), develop uniform standards and guidelines for Federal computers, except those systems excluded by section 2315 of title 10, United States Code, or section 3502(2) of title 44, United States Code;

"(3) have responsibility within the Federal Government for developing technical, management, physical, and administrative standards and guidelines for the cost-effective security and privacy of sensitive information in Federal computer systems except—

"(A) those systems excluded by section 2315 of title 10, United States Code, or section 3502(2) of title 44, United States Code; and

"(B) those systems which are protected at all times by procedures established for information which has been specifically authorized under criteria established by an Executive order or an Act of Congress to be kept secret in the interest of national defense or foreign policy, the primary purpose of which standards and guidelines shall be to control loss and unauthorized modification or disclosure of sensitive information in such systems and to prevent computer-related fraud and misuse;

"(4) submit standards and guidelines developed pursuant to paragraphs (2) and (3) of this subsection, along with recommendations as to the extent to which these should be made compulsory and binding, to the Secretary of Commerce for promulgation under section 111(d) of the Federal Property and Administrative Services Act of 1949;

"(5) develop guidelines for use by operators of Federal computer systems that contain sensitive information in training their employees in security awareness and accepted security practice, as required by section 5 of the Computer Security Act of 1987; and

"(6) develop validation procedures for, and evaluate the effectiveness of, standards and guidelines developed pursuant to paragraphs (1), (2), and (3) of this subsection through research and liaison with other government and private agencies.

"(b) In fulfilling subsection (a) of this section, the National Bureau of Standards is authorized—

"(1) to assist the private sector, upon request, in using and applying the results of the programs and activities under this section;

"(2) to make recommendations, as appropriate, to the Administrator of General Services on policies and regulations proposed pursuant to section 111(d) of the Federal Property and Administrative Services Act of 1949;

"(3) as requested, to provide to operators of Federal computer systems technical assistance in implementing the standards and guidelines promulgated pursuant to section 111(d) of the Federal Property and Administrative Services Act of 1949;

"(4) to assist, as appropriate, the Office of Personnel Management in developing regulations pertaining to training, as required by section 5 of the Computer Security Act of 1987;

"(5) to perform research and to conduct studies, as needed, to determine the nature and extent of the vulnerabilities of, and to devise techniques for the cost-effective security and privacy of sensitive information in Federal computer systems; and

"(6) to coordinate closely with other agencies and offices (Including, but not limited to, the Departments of Defense and Energy, the National Security Agency, and the General Accounting Office, the Office of Technology Assessment, and the Office of Management and Budget)—

"(A) to assure maximum use of all existing and planned programs, materials, studies, and reports relating to computer systems security and privacy, in order to avoid unnecessary and costly duplication of effort; and

"(B) to assure, to the maximum extent feasible, that standards developed pursuant to subsection (a)(3) and (5) are consistent and compatible with standards and procedures developed for the protection of information in Federal computer systems which is authorized under criteria established by Executive order or an Act of Congress to be kept secret in the interest of national defense or foreign policy.

"(c) For the purposes of—

"(1) developing standards and guidelines for the protection of sensitive information in Federal computer systems under subsections (a)(1) and (a)(3), and

"(2) performing research and conducting studies under subsection (b)(5), the National Bureau of Standards shall draw upon computer system technical security guidelines developed by the National Security Agency to the extent that the National Bureau of Standards determines that such guidelines are consistent with the requirements for protection of sensitive information in Federal computer systems.

"(d) As used in this section—

"(1) the term 'computer system'—

"(A) means any equipment or interconnected system or subsystems of equipment that is used in the automatic acquisition, storage, manipulation, management, movement, control, display, switching, interchange, transmission, or reception, of data or information; and

"(B) includes—

"(i) computers;

"(ii) ancillary equipment;

"(iii) software, firmware, or similar procedures;

"(iv) services, including support services;

"(v) related resources as defined by regulations issued by the Administrator for General Services pursuant to section 111 of the Federal Property and Administrative Services Act of 1949;

"(2) the term 'Federal computer system'—

"(A) means a computer system operated by a Federal agency or by a contractor of a Federal agency or other organization that processes information (using a computer system) on behalf of the Federal Government to accomplish a Federal function; and

"(B) includes automatic data processing equipment as that term is defined in section 111(a)(2) of the Federal Property and Administrative Services Act of 1949;

"(3) the term 'operator of a Federal computer system' means a Federal agency, contractor of a Federal agency, or other organization that processes information using a computer system on behalf of the Federal Government to accomplish a Federal function;

"(4) the term 'sensitive information' means any information, the loss, misuse, or unauthorized access to or modification of which could adversely affect the national interest or the conduct of Federal programs, or the privacy to which individuals are entitled under section 552a of title 5, United States Code (the Privacy Act), but which has not been specifically authorized under criteria established by an Executive order or an Act of Congress to be kept secret in the interest of national defense or foreign policy; and

"(5) the term 'Federal agency' has the meaning given such term by section 3(b) of the Federal Property and Administrative Services Act of 1949.

"Sec. 21. (a) There is hereby established a Computer System Security and Privacy Advisory Board within the Department of Commerce. The Secretary of Commerce shall appoint the chairman of the Board. The Board shall be composed of twelve additional members appointed by the Secretary of Commerce as follows:

"(1) four members from outside the Federal Government who are eminent in the computer or telecommunications industry, at least one of whom is representative of small or medium sized companies in such industries;

"(2) four members from outside the Federal Government who are eminent in the fields of computer or telecommunication technology, or related disciplines, but who are not employed or representative of a producer of computer or telecommunications equipment; and

"(3) four members from the Federal Government who have computer systems management experience, including experience in computer systems security and privacy, at least one of whom shall be from the National Security Agency.

"(b) The duties of the Board shall be—

"(1) to identify emerging managerial, technical, administrative, and physical safeguard issues relative to computer systems security and privacy;

"(2) to advise the Bureau of Standards and the Secretary of Commerce on security and privacy issues pertaining to Federal computer systems; and

"(3) to report its findings to the Secretary of Commerce, the Director of the Office of Management and Budget, the Director of the National Security Agency, and the appropriate committees of the Congress.

"(c) The term of office of each member of the Board shall be four years, except that—

"(1) of the initial members, three shall be appointed for terms of one year, three shall be appointed for terms of two years, three shall be appointed for terms of three years, and three shall be appointed for terms of four years; and

"(2) any member appointed to fill a vacancy in the Board shall serve for the remainder of the term for which his predecessor was appointed.

"(d) The board shall not act in the absence of a quorum, which shall consist of seven members.

"(e) Members of the Board, other than full-time employees of the Federal Government, while attending meetings of such committees or while otherwise performing duties at the request of the Board Chairman while away from their homes or a regular place of business, may be allowed travel expenses in accordance with subchapter I of chapter 57 of title 5, United States Code.

"(f) To provide the staff services necessary to assist the board in carrying out its functions, the Board may utilize personnel from the National Bureau of Standards or any other agency of the Federal Government with the consent of the head of the agency.

"(g) As used in this section, the terms 'computer system' and 'Federal computer system' have the meanings given in section 20(d) of this Act."; and

(3) by adding at the end thereof the following new section:

"Sec. 23. This Act may be cited as the National Bureau of Standards Act."

Sec. 4. Amendment To Brooks Act.

Section 111(d) of the Federal Property and Administrative Services Act of 1949 (40 U.S.C. 759(d)) is amended to read as follows:

"(d)(1) The Secretary of Commerce shall, on the basis of standards and guidelines developed by the National Bureau of Standards pursuant to section 20(a) (2) and (3) of the National Bureau of Standards Act, promulgate standards and guidelines pertaining to Federal computer systems, making such standards compulsory and binding to the extent to which the Secretary determines necessary to improve the efficiency of operation or security and privacy of Federal computer systems. The President may disapprove or modify such standards and guidelines if he determines such action to be in the public interest. The President's authority to disapprove or modify such standards and guidelines may not be delegated. Notice of such disapproval or modification shall be submitted promptly to the Committee on Government Operations of the House of Representatives and the Committee on Governmental Affairs of the Senate and shall be published promptly in the Federal Register. Upon receiving notice of such disapproval or modification, the Secretary of Commerce shall immediately rescind or modify such standards or guidelines as directed by the President.

"(2) The head of a Federal agency may employ standards for the cost-effective security and privacy of sensitive information in a Federal computer system within or under the supervision of that agency that are more stringent than the standards promulgated by the Secretary of Commerce, if such standards contain, at a minimum, the provisions of those applicable standards made compulsory and binding by the Secretary of Commerce.

"(3) The standards determined to be compulsory and binding may be waived by the Secretary of Commerce in writing upon a determination that compliance would adversely affect the accomplishment of the mission of an operator of a Federal computer system, or cause a major adverse financial impact on the operator which is not offset by Government-wide savings. The Secretary may delegate to the head of one or more Federal agencies authority to waive such standards to the extent to which the Secretary determines such action to be necessary and desirable to allow for timely and effective implementation of Federal computer systems standards. The head of such agency may redelegate such authority only to a senior official designated pursuant to section 3506(b) of title 44, United States Code. Notice of each such waiver and delegation shall be transmitted promptly to the Committee on Government Operations of the House of Representatives and the Committee on Governmental Affairs of the Senate and shall be published promptly in the Federal Register.

"(4) The administrator shall revise the Federal information resources management regulations (41 CFR ch. 201) to be consistent with the standards and guidelines promulgated by the Secretary of Commerce under this subsection.

"(5) As used in this subsection, the terms 'Federal computer system' and 'operator of a Federal computer system' have the meanings given in section 20(d) of the National Bureau of Standards Act."

Sec. 5. Federal Computer System Security Training.

(a) In General—Each Federal agency shall provide for the mandatory periodic training in computer security awareness and accepted computer security practice of all employees who are involved with the management, use, or operation of each Federal computer system within or under the supervision of that agency. Such training shall be—

(1) provided in accordance with the guidelines developed pursuant to section 20(a)(5) of the National Bureau of Standards Act (as added by section 3 of this Act), and in accordance with the regulations issued under subsection (c) of this section for Federal civilian employees; or

(2) provided by an alternative training program approved by the head of the agency on the basis of a determination that the alternative training program is at least as effective in accomplishing the objectives of such guidelines and regulations.

(b) Training Objectives—Training under this section shall be started within 60 days after the issuance of the regulations described in subsection (c). Such training shall be designed—

(1) to enhance employees' awareness of the threats to and vulnerability of computer systems; and

(2) to encourage the use of improved computer security practices.

(c) Regulations—Within six months after the date of the enactment of this Act, the Director of the Office of Personnel Management shall issue regulations prescribing the procedures and scope of the training to be provided Federal civilian employees under subsection (a) and the manner in which such training is to be carried out.

Sec. 6. Additional Responsibilities For Computer Systems Security and Privacy.

(a) Identification of Systems That Contain Sensitive Information—Within six months after the date of enactment of this Act, each Federal agency shall identify each Federal computer system, and system under development, which is within or under the supervision of that agency and which contains sensitive information.

(b) Security Plan—Within one year after the date of enactment of this Act, each such agency shall, consistent with the standards, guidelines, policies, and regulations prescribed pursuant to section 111(d) of the Federal Property and Administrative Services Act of 1949, establish a plan for the security and privacy of each Federal computer system identified by that agency pursuant to subsection (a) that is commensurate with the risk and magnitude of the harm resulting from the loss, misuse, or unauthorized access to or modification of the information contained in such a system. Copies of each such plan shall be transmitted to the National Bureau of Standards and the National Security Agency for advice and comment. A summary of such plan shall be included in the agency's five-year plan required by section 3505 of title 44, United States Code. Such plan shall be subject to disapproval by the Director of the Office of Management and Budget. Such plan shall be revised annually as necessary.

Sec. 7. Definitions.

As used in this Act, the terms "computer system," "Federal computer system," "operator or a Federal computer system," "sensitive information," and "Federal agency" have the meanings given in section 20(d) of the National Bureau of Standards Act (as added by section 3 of this Act.)

Sec. 8. Rules Of Construction Of Act.

Nothing in this Act, or in any amendment made by this Act, shall be construed—

(1) to constitute authority to withhold information sought pursuant to section 552 of title 5, United States Code; or

(2) to authorize any Federal agency to limit, restrict, regulate, or control the collection, maintenance, disclosure, use, transfer or sale of any information (regardless of the medium in which the information may be maintained) that is—

(A) privately-owned information;

(B) disclosable under section 552 of title 5, United States Code, or other law requiring or authorizing the public disclosure of information; or

(C) public domain information.

NOTES

1. Computer Security Act of 1987, Pub. L. No. 100-235, 101 Stat. 1724 (1987).

2. *The Computer Security Act of 1987: Hearings before the Subcommittee on Science, Research and Technology of the House of Representatives Committee on Science, Space and Technology*, 100th Cong., 1st Sess. 8 (1987).

3. John Horgan, "Civil defense: the military loses a fight for control of data—or does it?" *Scientific American 258: 18 (March 1988)*.

4. Jessica D. Schwab, *Government Publications Review* 17: 25 (1990).

Appendix C

Media Pools in the Persian Gulf 1991

In August of 1990, U.S. Navy Captain Ron Wildermuth prepared a ten-page memo outlining the kind of restrictions the U.S. Central Command office in Tampa, Florida, would impose on media representatives for the duration of the Persian Gulf military action.[1] This memo clearly spelled out the public information policy that the executive branch desired—to "manage the information flow in a way that supported the operation's [Desert Shield] goals and avoided the perceived mistakes of Vietnam."[2] The memo went on to stress, "News media representatives will be escorted at all times. Repeat, at all times."[3]

Some of the material supplied reporters by the U.S. military was later found to be false or intentionally misleading. Some examples are that in fact—contrary to what was originally released by administration sources—only about one weapon in ten was a precision-guided weapon,[4] and that a record one-third of the U.S. troop deaths resulted from "friendly fire."[5]

As late as mid-January 1991, some members of Congress urged action against the media pool system in place at the Pentagon. But at no time did Congress move to counteract or protest the Pentagon's media pool program made known to them specifically before the military strike in Kuwait.[6]

(April 13, 1990)
Ground Rules

You have been selected to participate as a member of the DoD National Media Pool. The ground rules below will protect the security

of the operation and the safety of the troops involved, while allowing
you the greatest permissible freedom and access in covering the story as
representatives of all U.S. media.

— Prior to your departure, do not tell anyone that the pool
has been activated. This is absolutely essential to preserve
security in the event of an actual contingency operation.

— You may not file stories or otherwise attempt to communi-
cate with any individual about the operation until stories
and all other information (from videotape, sound bites,
photo cutlines, etc.) have been pooled with other pool
members. This pooling may take place at a pool member
meeting during or immediately following the operation.
You will be expected to brief other pool members concerning your experiences. Detailed instructions on filing will
be provided by your military escorts at an appropriate
time.

— You must remain with the escort officers at all times, until
released—and follow their instructions regarding your
activities. These instructions are not intended to hinder
your reporting and are given only to facilitate movement
of the pool and ensure troop safety.

— Failure to follow these ground rules may result in your
expulsion from the pool.

Your participation in the pool indicates your understanding of these guidelines and your willingness to abide by
them.

Additional Ground Rules for the DoD National Media Pool for Operation Desert Shield

1. In addition to the standard DoD National Media pool ground
rules, the following ground rules will be enforced for Operation Desert
Shield.

A. The following categories of information are not releasable:
— Number of troops
— Number of aircraft
— Number of other equipment, e.g. artillery, tanks, radars,
trucks, water "buffaloes," etc.
— Names of military installations/geographic locations of
U.S. military units in Saudi Arabia

—   Information regarding future operations
—   Information concerning security precautions at military
    installations in Saudi Arabia
—   Names/hometowns of U.S. military personnel being inter-
    viewed, and names of Saudis being interviewed. Com-
    manders of U.S. units being interviewed are excepted from
    this provision.
—   Photography that would show level of security at military
    installations in Saudi Arabia
—   Photography that would reveal the name or specific loca-
    tion of military forces or installations.

2. If you are not sure whether an action you will take will violate a
ground rule, consult your escort officer PRIOR TO TAKING THAT
ACTION.

(December 13, 1990)
Operation Desert Shield
News Media Ground Rules

All interviews with service members will be on the record.
Security at the source is the policy. In the event of hostilities, media
products will be subject to security review prior to release. Interviews
with pilots and aircrew members are authorized upon completion of
mission; however, release of information must conform to the ground
rules stated below.

All Navy embark stories will state that the report is coming "from
the Persian Gulf, Red Sea or North Arabian Sea." Stories written in
Saudi Arabia may be datelined Riyadh, Dhahran, or other area by
general geographical description, such as "Eastern Saudi Arabia."
Stories from other participating countries may be datelined from those
countries only after their participation is released by DoD.

You must be physically fit. If, in the opinion of the commander,
you are unable to withstand the rigorous conditions required to operate
with his forward-deployed forces, you will be medically evacuated out
of the area.

You are not authorized to carry a personal weapon.

(January 14, 1991, revised from January 7 version)
Operation Desert Shield
Ground Rules

The following information should not reported because its publication or broadcast could jeopardize operations and endanger lives:

(1) For U.S. or coalition units, specific numerical information on troop strength, aircraft, weapons systems, on-hand equipment, or supplies (e.g., artillery, tanks, radars, missiles, trucks, water), including amounts of ammunitions or fuel moved by or on-hand in support and combat units. Unit size may be described in general terms such as "company-size," "multibattalion," "multidivision," "naval task force," and "carrier battle group." Number or amount of equipment and supplies may be described in general terms such as "large," "small," or "many."

(2) Any information that reveals details of further plans, operations, or strikes, including postponed or canceled operations.

(3) Information, photography, and imagery that would reveal the specific location of military forces or show the level of security at military installations or encampments. Locations may be described as follows: all Navy embark stories can identify the ship upon which embarked as a dateline and will state that the report is coming from the "Persian Gulf," "Red Sea," or "North Arabian Sea." Stories written in Saudi Arabia may be datelined "Eastern Saudi Arabia," "Near the Kuwaiti border," etc. For specific countries outside Saudi Arabia, stories will state that the report is coming from the Persian Gulf region unless that country has acknowledged its participation.

(4) Rules of engagement details.

(5) Information on intelligence collection activities, including targets, methods, and results.

(6) During an operation, specific information on friendly force troop movements, tactical deployments, and dispositions that would jeopardize operational security or lives. This would include unit designations, name of operations, and size of friendly forces involved, until release by CENTCOM.

(7) Identification of mission aircraft points or origin, other than as land- or carrier-based.

(8) Information on the effectiveness of enemy camouflage, cover, deception, targeting, direct or indirect fire, intelligence collection, or security measures.

(9) Specific identifying information on missing or downed aircraft or ships while search and rescue operations are planned or underway.

(10) Special Operations forces' methods, unique equipment or tactics.

(11) Specific operating methods and tactics (e.g., air angles of attack or speeds, or naval tactics and evasive maneuvers). General terms such as "low" or "fast" may be used.

(12) Information on operational or support vulnerabilities that could be used against U.S. Forces, such as details of major battle damage or major personnel losses of specific U.S. or coalition units, until that information no longer provides tactical advantage to the enemy and is, therefore, released by CENTCOM. Damage and casualties may be described as "light," "moderate," or "heavy."

Guidelines for News Media

News media personnel must carry and support any personal and professional gear they take with them, including protective cases for professional equipment, batteries, cables, converters, etc.

Night Operations—Light discipline restrictions will be followed. The only approved light source is a flashlight with a red lens. No visible light source, including flash or television lights, will be used when operating with forces at night unless specifically approved by the on-scene commander.

Because of host-nation requirements, you must stay with your public affairs escort while on Saudi bases. At other U.S. tactical or field locations and encampments, a public affairs escort may be required because of security, safety, and mission requirements as determined by the host commander.

Casualty information, because of concern of the notification of the next of kin, is extremely sensitive. By executive directive, next of kin of all military fatalities must be notified in person by a uniformed member of the appropriate service. There have been instances in which the next of kin have first learned of the death or wounding of a loved one through the news media. The problem is particularly difficult for visual media. Casualty photographs showing a recognizable face, name tag, or other identifying feature or item should not be used before the next of kin have been notified. The anguish that sudden recognition at home can cause far outweighs the news value of the photograph, film or videotape. News coverage of casualties in medical centers will be in strict compliance with the instructions of doctors and medical officials.

To the extent that individuals in the news media seek access to the U.S. arena of operation, the following rule applies: Prior to or upon commencement of hostilities, media pools will be established to provide initial combat coverage of U.S. forces. U.S. news media personnel present in Saudi Arabia will be given the opportunity to join CENTCOM media pools, providing they agree to pool their products. News media personnel who are not members of the official CENTCOM media pools will not be permitted into forward areas. Reporters are strongly discouraged from attempting to link up on their own with combat units. U.S. commanders will maintain extremely tight security throughout the operational area and will exclude from the area of operation all unauthorized individuals.

For news media personnel participating in designated CENTCOM Media Pools:

(1) Upon registering with the JIB, news media should contact their respective pool coordinator for an explanation of pool operations.

(2) In the event of hostilities, pool products will be the subject of review before release to determine if they contain sensitive information about military plans, capabilities, operations, or vulnerabilities (see attached ground rules) that would jeopardize the outcome of an operation or the safety of U.S. or coalition forces. Material will be examined solely for its conformance to the attached ground rules, not for its potential to express criticism or cause embarrassment. The public affairs escort officer on scene will review pool reports, discuss ground rule problems with the reporter, and in the limited circumstances when no agreement can be reached with a reporter about disputed materials, immediately send the disputed materials to the JIB Dhahran for review by the JIB Director and the appropriate news media representative. If no agreement can be reached, the issue will be immediately forwarded to OASD(PA) for review with the appropriate bureau chief. The ultimate decision on publication will be made by the originating reporter's news organization.

(3) Correspondents may not carry a personal weapon.

NOTES

1. "Annex Foxtrot," from the office of Ron Wildermuth, memo dated August 1990, cited by *The New York Times*, May 5, 1991, A1.

2. *The New York Times*, May 5, 1991, A1.

3. *The New York Times*, May 5, 1991.

4. "Pentagon Acknowledges Some of its Bombs Killing Civilians," Associated Press, February 13, 1991.

5. "U.S. Works to Cut 'Friendly Fire' Deaths," Associated Press, December 9, 1991.

6. *House of Representatives Armed Services Committee Hearings*, January 16-17, 1991.

Selected Bibliography

PRIMARY SOURCES

U.S. Congress. House. Committee on Foreign Affairs and the Joint Economic Committee. *The Persian Gulf Crisis: Joint Hearings Before the Subcommittee on Arms Control, International Security and Science, Europe and the Middle East, and on International Operations.* 101st Cong., 2d Sess. 1990.

U.S. Congress. House. Committee on Government Operations. *Military and Civilian Controls of Computer Security Issues: Hearing Before the Legislation and National Security Subcommittee.* 101st Cong., 1st Sess. 1989.

U.S. Congress. House. Committee on the Judiciary. *Foreign Communications Free Trade Act of 1989: Hearings Before the Subcommittee on Courts, Intellectual Property and the Administration of Justice.* 101st Cong., 2d Sess. 1990.

U.S. Congress. House. Committee on the Judiciary. *Free Trade in Ideas: Hearings Before the Subcommittee on Courts, Intellectual Property, and the Administration of Justice.* 101st Cong., 1st Sess. 1989.

U.S. Congress. House. Committee on the Judiciary. *Modification of the Foreign Agents Registration Act of 1938: Hearings Before the Subcommittee on Administrative Law and Governmental Relations.* 102d Cong., 1st Sess. 1991.

U.S. Congress. House. Committee on Science, Space, and Technology. *The Computer Security Act of 1987: Hearings Before the Subcommittee on Science, Research and Technology.* 100th Cong., 1st Sess. 1987.

U.S. Congress. House. Committee on Science, Space, and Technology. *Implementation of the Computer Security Act: Hearing Before the Subcommittee on Transportation, Aviation and Materials.* 100th Cong., 2d Sess. 1988.

U.S. Congress. House. Committee on Science, Space and Technology. *Implementation of the Computer Security Act: Hearing Before the Subcommittee on Transportation, Aviation and Materials.* 101st Cong., 1st Sess. 1989.

U.S. Congress. House. Committee on Science, Space and Technology. *Implementation of the Computer Security Act: Hearing Before the Subcommittee on Transportation, Aviation and Materials.* 101st Cong., 2d Sess. 1990.

U.S. Congress. House. Committee on Science, Space and Technology. *Computer Security: Hearings Before the Subcommittee on Technology and Competitiveness.* 102d Cong., 1st Sess. 1991.

U.S. Congress. House. Special Subcommittee on Government Information. *Availability of the Information from Federal Departments and Agencies.* 84th Cong., 1st Sess., 7 November 1955.

U.S. Congress. Senate. Committee on Armed Services. *Crisis in the Persian Gulf Region: U.S. Policy Options and Implications.* 101st Cong., 2d Sess. 1990.

U.S. Congress. Senate. Committee on Commerce, Science, and Transportation. *Foreign Influence in the United States.* 101st Cong., 2d Sess. 1990.

U.S. Congress. Senate. Committee on Governmental Affairs. *Federal Lobbying Disclosure Laws: Hearings Before the Subcommittee on Oversight of Government Management of the Senate Committee on Governmental Affairs.* 102d Cong., 1st Sess. 1991.

U.S. Congress. Senate. Committee on Governmental Affairs. *Pentagon Rules on Media Access to the Persian Gulf War.* 102d Cong., 1st Sess. 1991.

U.S. Department of Justice. *Department of Justice Report on Electronic Record Issues Under the Freedom of Information Act.* GPO October 1990.

U.S. Department of Justice. *Freedom of Information Case List.* GPO September 1991 and 1992.

SECONDARY SOURCES

Adler, Mortimer J. *We Hold These Truths: Understanding the Ideas and Ideals of the Constitution.* New York: Macmillan, 1987.

Alexander, Michael. "Hacker's Paradise?" *Computerworld.* August 12, 1991, special section pp.S26-27.

Altschull, J. Herbert. *From Milton to McLuhan.* New York: Longman, 1990.

Bagdikian, Ben H. *The Information Machines: Their Impact on Men and the Media.* New York: Harper, 1971.

Baker, C. Edwin. *Human Liberty and Freedom of Speech.* New York: Oxford University Press, 1989.

Benecki, Maria H. "Developments Under the Freedom of Information Act—1987." *Duke Law Journal* 1988: 566, 1988.

Beniger, James. *Control Revolution: Technology and Economic Origins of the Information Society.* Cambridge, Mass.: Harvard University Press, 1986.

Berman, Jerry J. "The Right to Know: Public Access to Electronic Public Information," *Software Law Journal* 3: 491 (1989).

Billington, James H. "The Electronic Library." Columbia University (New York): The Freedom Forum Media Studies Center: Media Studies Journal. Winter 1994, 109-112.

Blanchard, Margaret A. *Revolutionary Sparks: Freedom of Expression In Modern America*. New York: Oxford University Press, 1992.

Blasi, Vincent. "The Checking Value in First Amendment Theory." 1977 *American Bar Foundation Research Journal* 523.

Bok, Sissela. *Lying: Moral Choice in Public and Private Life*. New York: Vintage, 1978.

Bok, Sissela. *Secrets: On the Ethics of Concealment and Revelation*. New York: Vintage, 1983.

Branscomb, Anne Wells. *Who Owns Information: From Privacy to Public Access*. New York: Basic Books, 1994.

Braverman, Burt and Frances J. Chetwynd. *Information Law: Freedom of Information, Privacy, Open Meetings, Other Access Laws*. New York: Practising Law Institute, 1990 supplement.

Brooker, Gregory G. "FOIA Exemption 3 and the CIA." *Minnesota Law Review* 68: 1231 (1984).

Brown, Richard D. *Knowledge Is Power: The Diffusion of Information in Early America, 1700-1865*. New York: Oxford University Press, 1989.

Brucker, Herbert. *Freedom of Information*. New York: Macmillan, 1949.

Buckland, Michael K. "Information as Thing." *Journal of the American Society for Information Science*. 42:351-360 (June 1991).

Cate, Fred H., Annette Fields, and James K. McBain. "The Right to Privacy and the Public's Right to Know: The 'Central Purpose' of the Freedom of Information Act," *Administrative Law Review* 46: 41 (Winter 1994).

Cate, Fred H., ed. *Visions of the First Amendment for a New Millennium*. Washington, D.C.: The Annenberg Washington Program in Communications Policy Studies of Northwestern University, 1992.

Chamberlin, Bill F., and Charlene Brown, eds. *The First Amendment Reconsidered*. New York: Longman, 1982.

Chick, Morey J. "Automated information security will not improve until effectively supported by IRM." *Information Management Review*. 5:29-36 (1989).

Christians, Clifford G., Kim B. Rotzoll, and Mark Fackler. *Media Ethics: Cases and Moral Reasoning*, 2d ed. New York: Longman, 1987.

Clement, John. "Sensitive (but unclassified)," *Bulletin of the American Society for Information Science* 13:14 (April-May 1987).

Cohen, Elliott D., ed. *Philosophical Issues in Journalism*. New York: Oxford University Press, 1992.

Curry, Richard O., ed. *Freedom at Risk*. Philadelphia: Temple University Press, 1988.

Dawson, Lynn Alvey. "Freedom of Expression—The Foreign Agents Registration Act, *Meese v. Keene.*" *Suffolk Transnational Law Journal* 12: 457 (1989).

Demac, Donna A. *Keeping America Uninformed.* New York: Pilgrim Press, 1984.

Dorsen, Norman, ed. *The Evolving Constitution.* Middletown, Conn.: Wesleyan University Press, 1987.

Ducat, Craig R. and Harold W. Chase. *Constitutional Interpretation* 4th ed. New York: West Publishing, 1988.

Du Mont, Rosemary Ruhig. "Ethics in Librarianship: A Management Model." *Library Trends* 40:201-215 (Fall 1991).

Dunn, Christopher. "Judging Secrets." *Villanova Law Review* 31: 471 (1986).

Dwivedi, O.P. and Joseph G. Jabbra, eds. *Public Service Accountability.* West Hartford, Conn.: Kumarian Press, 1988.

Dworkin, R.M., ed. *The Philosophy of Law.* New York: Oxford University Press, 1979.

Emerson, Thomas. "Toward a General Theory of the First Amendment. *Yale Law Journal* 72: 877 (1963).

Fialka, John J. *Hotel Warriors.* Baltimore: The Woodrow Wilson Center Press, 1992.

Foerstel, Herbert. *Secret Science: Federal Control of American Science and Technology.* Westport, Conn.: Praeger, 1993.

Foerstel, Herbert. *Surveillance in the Stacks: The FBI's Library Awareness Program.* Westport, Conn.: Praeger, 1991.

Forester, Tom and Perry Morrison. *Computer Ethics.* Cambridge, Mass.: MIT Press, 1990.

Forester, Tom, ed. *The Information Technology Revolution.* Cambridge, Mass.: MIT Press, 1985.

Gerard, David, ed. *Libraries in Society.* New York: Clive Bingley, 1978.

Goodwin, H. Eugene. *Groping for Ethics in Journalism.* Ames: Iowa State University Press, 1987.

Hammitt, Harry. "FOIA suffering from restrictive new court rulings." *The Quill* 79:30 (October 1991).

Hammond, William M. "The Army and Public Affairs: A Glance Back," in *Newsmen & National Defense: Is Conflict Inevitable?* New York: Macmillan, 1991.

Hocking, William E. *Freedom of the Press: A Framework of Principle.* Chicago: University of Chicago Press, 1947.

Hoffman, Fred S. *Review of Panama Pool Deployment, December 1989.* Washington, D.C.: Department of Defense, 1990.

Holden, Constance. "Animal Rightists Raid USDA Lab." *Science* 237:1099 (September 4, 1987).

Holsinger, Ralph. *Media Law.* New York: Random House, 1987.

Horgan, John. "Civil defense: the military loses a fight for control of data—or does it?" *Scientific American* 258:18 (March 1988).

Hughes, Michael H. "CIA v.Sims: Supreme Court Deference to Agency Interpretation of FOIA Exemption 3." *Catholic University Law Review* 35: 279
(1985).

Journals, ed. Library of Congress, 5 (September 26, 1776): 829; 8 (June 2,
1777): 412.

Kammen, Michael, ed. *The Origins of the American Constitution*. New York:
Penguin Books, 1986.

Kant, Immanuel. *Critique of Pure Reason*. Translated by J.M.D. Meiklejohn.
Chicago, Illinois: University of Chicago Press, 1952.

Katsh, M. Ethan. *The Electronic Media and the Transformation of Law*. New
York: Oxford University Press, 1989.

Knightly, Phillip. *The First Casualty*. New York: Harcourt Brace Jovanovich,
1975.

Kostyu, Paul E. "Partners in the Freedom of Information Movement: The
Press and John E. Moss, Jr." Paper presented to the Association for
Education of Journalism and Mass Communication conference, August
1991, Boston, Mass.

"Labeling Canadian Films 'Propaganda' Does Not Infringe Freedom of
Speech." *The News Media and the Law* 11:14-16 (Summer 1987).

Lacy, Dan M. "Libraries and the Freedom of Access to Information," in
Libraries and the Life of the Mind in America, ed. Edward G. Holley.
Chicago: American Library Association, 1977.

Lacy, Dan M. "Social Change and the Library: 1945-1980," in *Libraries at
Large*, ed. Douglas M. Knight and E. Shepley Nourse. New York: R.R.
Bowker, 1969.

LaRue, James. "Micro Biology." *Wilson Library Bulletin* 65:88-133 (September
1990).

Leigh, Robert D. *The Public Library in the United States*. New York: Columbia
University Press, 1950.

Lesser, Barry. "Information Protection Issues in the Information Economy."
Bulletin of the American Society for Information Science 14:21-22
(February/March 1988).

Lichtenberg, Judith, ed. *Democracy and the Mass Media*. New York: Cambridge University Press, 1990.

Lippmann, Walter. *Public Opinion*. New York: Harcourt, Brace & Co., 1922.

Lipschultz, Jeremy Harris. "Political Propaganda: The Supreme Court Decision in *Meese v. Keene*." *Communications and the Law* 11: 25 (December
1989).

Locke, John. *Concerning Civil Government, Second Essay*. 1694.

MacArthur, John. *Second Front: Censorship and Propaganda in the Gulf War*.
New York: Hill and Wang, 1992.

Meiklejohn, Alexander. *Free Speech and Its Relation to Self-Government*. New
York: Harper, 1948.

Meyer, Philip. *Ethical Journalism*. New York: Longman, 1987.

Mill, John Stuart. *Representative Government*. 1861.

Mill, John Stuart. *Utilitarianism*. 1863.

Miller, Sarah Jordan. *The Depository Library System: A History*. Columbia University dissertation. 1980.

Morawetz, Thomas. *The Philosophy of Law*. New York: Macmillan, 1980.

Mulgan, G.J. *Communication and Control*. New York: The Guilford Press, 1991.

Nagy, Alex. "Word Wars at Home: U.S. Response to World War II Propaganda." *Journalism Quarterly* 67:207-213 (Spring 1990).

O'Reilly, James R. *Federal Information Disclosure*, 2d ed. Colorado Springs, Colorado: Sheppard's/McGraw-Hill, 1990.

Overbeck, Wayne and Rick D. Pullen. *Major Principles of Media Law*. New York: Holt, Rinehart and Winston, 1985.

Paredes-Japa, Divina. "Bush flexes secrecy muscles." *The Quill* 79:28 (October 1991).

Peterson, I. "The complexity of computer security," *Science News* 134:199 (September 24, 1988).

Pia, J. Joseph. "Information Security." *Bulletin for the American Society of Information Science*. 13:16-17 (April/May 1987).

Plakins, Ava Marion. "Political Propaganda." *Fordham International Law Journal* 11: 187-207 (1987).

"Poll on Privacy." *Time* 138:36 (November 11, 1991).

Popkin, James. "Running the new, improved FOIA obstacle course." *Columbia Journalism Review* 28:45 (July-August 1989).

Raloff, Janet. "Coming: The Big Chill?" *Science News* 131:314 (May 16, 1987).

Rogers, Everett M. and F. Floyd Shoemaker. *Communication of Innovations* 2d ed. New York: Collier-Macmillan, 1971.

Roumfort, Susan. "Just when you think everything is okay—the continuing need to protect confidential library records." *Education Libraries* 13:36-38 (Spring/Fall 1988).

Ruben, Brent, ed. *Information and Behavior*. New Brunswick, N.J.: Transaction, 1988.

Schauer, Frederick. *Free Speech: A Philosophical Enquiry*. Cambridge: University of Cambridge Press, 1982.

Schmidt, Benno C., Jr. *Freedom of the Press vs. Public Access*. New York: Praeger Publishers, 1976.

Schmuhl, Robert. "The Road to Responsibility," in *The Responsibilities of Journalism*. Notre Dame, Indiana: University of Notre Dame Press, 1984.

Schwab, Jessica D. "National Security Restraints of the Federal Government On Academic Freedom and Scientific Communication in the United States." *Government Publications Review* 17:17 (1990).

Sharkey, Jacqueline. *Under Fire: U.S. Military Restrictions on the Media from Grenada to the Persian Gulf*. Washington, D.C.: The Center for Public Integrity, 1991.

Shera, Jesse H. *Foundations of the Public Library: The Origins of the Public Library Movement in New England 1629-1855*. Chicago, Illinois: University of Chicago Press, 1949.

Siebert, Fredrick S. *Freedom of the Press in England 1476-1776*. Urbana: University of Illinois, 1952.

Simpson, Jack W. "Online Industry Spearheads Effort to Curb Government Control of Information," *Online* 11:7 (July 1987).

Sims, Calvin. "What Price Convenience: New Devices Can Reveal A Lot." *New York Times* November 3, 1991, 5(E).

Smolla, Rodney A. *Free Speech in an Open Society*. New York: Vintage, 1992.

Smolla, Rodney A. and Stephen A. Smith. "Propaganda, Xenophobia and the First Amendment." *Oregon Law Review* 67: 253-285 (1988).

Soma, John T. and Elizabeth J. Bedient. "Computer security and the protection of sensitive but not classified data." *Air Force Law Review* 30: 135 (1989).

Sorokin, Leo T. "The Computerization of Government Information: Does It Circumvent Public Access Under the Freedom of Information Act and the Depository Library Program," *Columbia Journal of Law and Social Problems* 24: 266 (1991).

Urofsky, Melvin I. *A March of Liberty: A Constitutional History of the United States* Vol. II: *Since 1865*. New York: Alfred A. Knopf, 1988.

Vagianos, Louis and Barry Lesser. "Information Policy Issues: Putting Library Policy in Context," in *Rethinking the Library in the Information Age*, Vol. II. Washington, D.C.: U.S. Department of Education, 1989.

Verduce, Valerie M. "*Meese v. Keene*: An Attempt to Keep the First Amendment from Raining on the Congressional Parade." *Southwestern University Law Review* 17: 373-408 (1987).

Waters, Robert G. "The Foreign Agents Registration Act: How Open Should the Marketplace of Ideas Be?" *Missouri Law Review* 53: 795-806 (1988).

White, Morton. *Philosophy, The Federalist and the Constitution*. New York: Oxford University Press, 1987.

Wiggins, James Russell. *Freedom or Secrecy*. New York: Oxford University Press, 1956.

Williams, Frederick and John V. Pavilk, eds. *The People's Right to Know: Media, Democracy, and the Information Highway*. Hillsdale, New Jersey: Erlbaum, 1994.

Wilson, Stan Le Roy. *Mass Media/Mass Culture*. New York: Random House, 1989.

Wurman, Richard Saul. *Information Anxiety*. New York: Doubleday, 1989.

Yerkey, A. Neil. "Password Protection for dBASE Applications." *Microcomputers for Information Management* 6:33-45 (March 1989).

Index

Abbotts v. Nuclear Regulatory Commission, 58
access, 1, 2, 4, 9, 55, 56, 59, 71, 77, 79, 93, 112; media, 72-74, 76, 86, 95; public, 8, 11, 30; right of, 10
Access, Pentagon Rules on Media, 4, 71-80
Adler, Mortimer J., 109
Aines, Andrew A., 25
Amend Federal Election Campaign Act, 96
Amendment, First, 2, 100, 111
American Library Association, 11, 66
American Society for Information Science, 61

Baker, Howard, Jr., 41
Baucus, Sen. Max, 48
Becker, Joseph, 32
Belkin, Nicholas, 24, 25, 32
Benecki, Maria H., 68
Beniger, James, 30
Berman, Jerry, 64, 106
Black, Justice Hugo, 38, 102
Blackmun, Justice Harry A., 103
Blanchard, Margaret, 5
Blasi, Vincent, 5, 90

Boxer, Rep. Barbara, 76
Braestrup, Peter, 80
Brooker, Gregory G., 68
Brookes, Bertram C., 23
Brucker, Herbert, 96
Buckland, Michael K., 24
Bush, Vannevar, 20

Campbell, Rep. Tom, 64
Case-Zablocki Act, 75
Cass, Ronald, 89
Chafee, Zechariah, 5
Chartrand, Robert Lee, 26
Chamberlin, Bill F., 96
Christians, Clifford, 97
Colero, Rep. Tony, 73
Computer Security Act, 1-3, 55, 93, 105, 112, 113
Computer Security Research and Training Act of, 1985 59
computer, virus, 65
Conyers, Rep. John, 63
Cooper, Kent, 80

data, defined, 23
Demac, Donna, 68
DeMey, Marc, 20

Depository Library Act, 9
Depository Library Program, 7
Douglas, William, 31
Dunn, Christopher, 6, 57

Edwards, Rep. Don, 42
Eisenhower, Gen. Dwight D., 78
Electronic Freedom of Information
    Improvement Act, 55
Emerson, Thomas, 89
EPA v. Mink, 58
Executive Order No. 12,065, 68
Executive Order No. 12,356, 58

Falkland War, 72
Fialka, John J., 80
films, Canadian, 42
First Amendment, 2, 100, 111
Foreign Agents Registration Act, 1-3,
    35, 37, 91, 102, 103, 112, 113
Foreign Communications Free Trade
    Act, 53
Foreign Lobbying and Propaganda
    Act, 41
foreign principal, 38
Fox, Christopher J., 23
Frankena, William K., 97
Freedom of Information Act, 2, 7, 9,
    55, 56
Freedom of Information Act,
    Exemption 1, 56, 57
Freedom of Information Act,
    Exemption 3, 56, 58
Fricker, Richard L., 57, 68
Friendly, Fred W., 96
Fulbright, J. William, 39

Garfield, Eugene, 22
Gitlow v. New York, 109
Glenn, Sen. John, 41, 76
Glickman, Rep. Dan, 46, 60
Goodwin, H. Eugene, 97
Gottschalk, Jack A., 81
Grenada war, 73, 94, 107
Guarini, Rep. Frank J., 48, 105

Hamilton, Rep. Lee, 12, 74, 75
Hammond, William M., 80
Harmon, Glynn, 31
Hayes, Robert M., 32
Hernon, Peter, 30
Hoffman, Fred S., 80, 81
Holmes, Justice Oliver Wendell, 101,
    102
Holsinger, Ralph, 98
Honduran war, 73
Hughes, Michael H., 58
Humphrey, Hubert H., 39, 41
Humpries, Arthur A., 81

information, 56; access to, 11, 85, 86,
    89, 94, 95; carrier, 30, 35, 40, 44,
    45, 72-74, 78, 79, 80, 86, 92, 93,
    95, 100, 103, 105-107, 111-113,
    115; classification, 62, 105;
    classified, 68; computer, 12, 14,
    55, 94; content, 30, 35, 36, 40, 44,
    45, 49, 60, 72-75, 77-80, 86, 92-95,
    100, 103, 105-107, 111-113, 115;
    control, 4, 5, 71, 72, 75, 85, 86, 89,
    91, 93-96, 99, 103, 105, 106, 108,
    111-115; as data, 22; definition,
    19; distribution, 19; flow, 2-4, 11,
    72, 86, 99, 103, 106, 108, 111,
    112, 115; government, 10, 65, 93,
    94; as knowledge, 23; legal, 26;
    protection, 26, 114; science, 19;
    sensitive, 59-62, 64, 93, 94, 105,
    106; shared, 104; society, 22;
    unclassified, 59, 64

Javits, Jacob, 41
Johnson, Rep. Tim, 48

Kammen, Michael, 109
Kant, Immanuel, 87, 92
Kaptur, Rep. Marcy, 47
Kastenmeier, Rep. Robert, 45, 104
Keene, Barry, 43
Knightley, Phillip, 80
knowledge, defined, 23

Kochen, Manfred, 24, 31

Lacy, Dan M., 11
Leahy, Sen. Patrick J., 55
Lesser, Barry, 26
Levine, Peter, 46, 104
Levy, Leonard W., 109
Lichtenberg, Judith, 108
Lilley, Dorothy B., 30
Locke, John, 108

MacArthur, John R., 80
Machlup, Fritz, 30
Madison, James, 99
Maine, Sir Henry Sumner, 109
Matthews, Lloyd J., 80
McCormack, John W., 37
McGovern, George, 41
Meese v. Keene, 35, 109
Meiklejohn, Alexander, 89
Mill, John Stuart, 88, 90, 92, 101
Miller, Gordon, 21
misinformation, 105
Moynihan, Sen. Daniel Patrick, 67

Nagy, Alex, 50
National Security, Decision Directive
    145, 59
New York Times v. United States, 109

Panama war, 73, 74, 94, 107
Paperwork Reduction Act, 13
Pentagon Media Rules, 3, 71, 95, 106,
    112, 113
Persian Gulf War, 71, 74, 107
Plakins, Ava Marion, 52
Poindexter Directive, 59
pools, media, 1, 3, 71, 73, 74, 77-79,
    95
Popper, Karl R., 23
Privacy Act, 62
Program, Depository Library, 2
propaganda, 35, 37, 40, 43, 46, 91;
    political, 42, 45; purposes, 37

records: electronic, 55; government,
    13
Regular Reports to Congress on Costs
    Act, 82
right to know, 10, 12, 77, 78, 99
rights, natural, 100, 111, 115
Ritchie, L. David, 21, 31
Ritter, Rep. Don, 65
Robertson, Stephen E., 24, 25, 32
Rosenberg, Victor, 25
Roth, Sen. William, 76
Ruben, Brent, 30

Schauer, Frederick, 5, 89
Schement, Jorge, 30
Schenck v. United States, 109
Schmidt, Benno C., 96
Schwartau, Winn, 65
security: classification, 11; computer,
    60, 65; national, 10, 12, 55, 56, 59,
    93, 95, 106
Sharkey, Jacqueline, 80
Shauer, Frederick, 46
Shaw, Donald L., 83
Sidle, Major Gen. Winant, 78, 82
Simpson, Jack W., 59
Sims v. CIA, 58
Smith, Adam, 7
Smith, Jeffery A., 109
Smolla, Rodney A., 53
Sommers, Christina Hoff, 97
speech: carrier, 104; content, 104
Stevens, Justice John Paul, 102
Stewart, Justice Potter, 96
Stoll, Clifford, 64
Stone, Chief Justice Harlan, 38
Stonier, Tom, 24
Summers, Harry G., 78, 107
Summers, Robert E., 81
Surprenant, Thomas T., 26
Swain, Bruce M., 97

Thurmond, Sen. Strom, 75
Trade Secrets Act, 58
Turn, Rein, 26

Urofsky, Melvin I., 109

Verduce, Valerie M., 50
Viereck v. United States, 38
Vietnam War, 72

Walden, Ruth, 97
war, in Grenada, 71
war, in Panama, 71
Water, Robert G., 53
Weiss, Rep. Ted, 74
White, Morton, 108
Wiggins, James Russell, 80, 81
Wildermuth, Ron 5
World War II, 78

About the Author

SHANNON E. MARTIN is an Assistant Professor in the Department of Journalism and Mass Media at Rutgers University in New Jersey. She has contributed to journals such as *Communication and the Law* and *Journalism Quarterly*.